MW01224673

Neighbouring for *Life*

Rick Abma

edited by Christy Janssens

ISBN: 978-1-4834-5704-8 (sc)
ISBN: 978-1-4834-8897-4 (hc)
ISBN: 978-1-4834-5703-1 (e)

Library of Congress Control Number: 2016917596

Because of the dynamic nature of the Internet, any web addresses or links contained in
this book may have changed since publication and may no longer be valid. The views
expressed in this work are solely those of the author and do not necessarily reflect the
views of the publisher, and the publisher hereby disclaims any responsibility for them.

Any people depicted in stock imagery provided by Thinkstock are models,
and such images are being used for illustrative purposes only.
Certain stock imagery © Thinkstock.

Lulu Publishing Services rev. date: 11/11/2018

CONTENTS

A Note About the Cover Art

"What happens behind closed doors is anyone's guess. We carry stories: we carry secrets. All the while, we live side-by-side in our neighbourhoods. It is very possible to live our lives hidden and unknown, our public faces being the only ones we know. And yet, everyone holds echoes of something greater - a destiny, an overarching story that creates a yearning in each one of us. How well do we recognize that in one another? Perhaps it is one of the greatest challenges with living in community, this recognition of a "bigger truth".....because the solitary guy putzing in his garage, the elderly lady who rarely smiles, the family that yells - are all so *unremarkable*. Imagine the rumours of glory that angels whisper over these same individuals - including you - because they know what God sees. How differently we would see one another! This is the larger story that guides the one who loves well, who lives fully present in the place where he finds himself..... the story of the Way where a red river ever flows with love for all."

Karen Tamminga-Paton, artist

Karen's imagery comes from the unfolding story she lives and, as a result, her work has a narrative quality with liberal use of visual metaphors. She enjoys the conversation between the artist, the art, and the viewer. Karen and her husband live in the beautiful Crowsnest Pass where she is mom, teacher and artist.

Alberta Society of Artists (full member) - Crowsnest Pass, Alberta

A Word from the Author

A few words to whet your appetite.

My role in writing this book is not because I wanted to be an author, but because I chose to go down a life path that would hopefully cure my curiosity and discover reality in the life God has given me. The idea of applying this discovery in one's neighbourhood seemed ideal, for not only has God given us the role of loving our neighbours, some have come to realize the value and importance that this has in life! And so I tried to live life more intentionally in my neighbourhood, motivated by Jesus' words, 'love your neighbour' and found a number of people who were willing to do the same in their neighbourhood. And then the stories started to come; stories that were not fabricated or manipulated, but stories that showed where God is at work, breathing life into people and places. And so I have filled this book with those stories that may help you catch the vision of life in the neighbourhood. Here's one:

"The day our house burned down, I knew things were going to change. We lived in our house for four and a half years. Then one July morning, we lost everything, so we had to move out of our great neighbourhood for one year. I always organized activities so we could get to know people more and draw closer together. I never realized how much we needed our neighbourhood until that year. They were there for us, for all of our needs, giving us food, clothing, money and mental support.

When Halloween came around that fall, we decided to come back to our empty lot and be there with our support group. We set up a table with candy bags, coffee and cookies for the adults. We had such an amazing time getting to see the children plus also getting to know the adults more. It turned out to be a night of sitting around our table and visiting with the neighbours for a long time while their children went door to door and later came back to get their mom and dad at our house. We had such a great time and the neighbours were so happy we came to be with them that night, even when we didn't have a house to be at. So the next Halloween when we were back in our house, we served in our driveway again to get that connection with new neighbours that moved in while we were gone.

We are so thankful for our great neighbourhood that we live in. If we never got out of our box to get to know them, we would have never known how much we needed each other.

Always keep praying to God to show you how to step out of your comfort zone to reach out to your neighbourhood . You will be amazed at how much you can do with God's help!"

As I travel around, I hear recurring statements regarding the vision of Neighbourhood Life. Outside of the regular fears and business (or busyness) that keep us from engaging in neighbouring, some of those recurring statements make it sound like this is something that can be 'checked off the list'. Sometimes the 'to do list' in regards to our neighbours can be unhelpful, causing us to think of our neighbours as a project that can be completed one day.

One helpful comment came one night as twenty of us gathered from our respective neighbourhoods to discuss how we can put on the "flesh" of Jesus (incarnate) just as God did when He sent Jesus into the world. The comment came in the form of a confession in which "loving your neighbour" would not be treated as an "addition" to the many things that we have to do in life, but as something that is part of our rhythm of life.

When it comes to loving our neighbours, I suppose it is much like loving a child; it is best when done out of unconditional love.

- Rick Abma

PART ONE

Pieces

A number of years ago, when I was a youth pastor, a few other youth pastors and I organized an event with the intention of encouraging our youth to become more discipled. The project took place over one weekend and the aim was to build confidence and direction within the teens. We wanted them to understand more about discipleship and more about themselves by helping them explore their strengths and equipping them with practical tools to use these strengths in their daily lives. The youth were divided up according to a specific gift they wanted to develop and placed in a group with a leader who also had this gift. The outline of the weekend was to spend time studying our gifts in the context of scripture, and then move out into our city to practically apply what we had learned.

My particular gift was hospitality and my group included seven other teens who had discerned that hospitality might be their gift as well. We spent the first part of the weekend studying this theme in the scriptures through various stories and applications. On Saturday afternoon, the time came for us to go out into the city and practically engage what we had been learning. As we were leaving the church, I noticed a sign above the doorway, announcing: "You are now entering the mission field." I'd seen signs like this before, and they always made me wonder what people actually thought when they encountered this message. What did that actually mean? It seemed so vague to me.

The first place I took the teens was a restaurant. We wanted to observe how a server or a waitress used their gifts of hospitality in welcoming and serving us. During our discussion over the meal, we made some notes about what hospitality meant in this context. Our next stop was the hospital. As we walked through the halls, I noticed that a few of the students were taking notes and trying to understand the components that made up this word, "hospitality." This project seemed to be working: we had studied the scriptures, we had discerned who we were, and now we were observing it in a real world context.

The last place we visited was a soup kitchen. I had arranged this ahead of time and, right before we left the hospital, I made sure that all the youth had a sheet of questions, which were intended to be a launching pad to spark connections with the people we were about to encounter. When we entered the soup kitchen, I noticed the anxiety level rising among the youth, even though I had explained to them exactly what was going to happen. There were about seven or eight people scattered amongst the chairs in the room and our group stood by the door, looking out over the room, evaluating what exactly we had gotten ourselves into. All of our intense study over the weekend was pointing toward this moment of application, which I thought was very doable. We had studied the scriptures, we had seen it all in action at the restaurant and the hospital, and we had discussed the worksheet that they had brought along with them. Now we were standing in a room with real people. It was time to act. I turned to the group and said: "Go."

Nobody moved.

Eventually, I took initiative and led the way; however, at that moment, I realized that there is a gap that exists for us between being a disciple and the actual idea of "going."

This story crossed my mind as I was driving to preach a message I had been asked to give on the theme of neighbouring. At that time, the idea of discipleship within the neighbourhood was an interesting subject to the people in the area where I live. I kept getting asked to preach and teach in various places, always on this theme. As I drove to the church, I thought about the youth in the soup kitchen and what it meant to be sent, or told by your leader to "go" after undergoing a great deal of preparation and study. I knew that I had to give a children's message during the service that morning, and I decided to forgo my original plans for the message in favour of an idea that formed in my mind from the story of those youth in the soup kitchen.

At church, when the time for the children's message came, I stood up and told all of the children to gather around. I asked for a volunteer and, among the eager flurry of raised hands, I picked a girl who seemed to be the most confident of the group. She stood up and I simply asked her to "go" before taking my seat again. Even though this girl was confident, she suddenly looked insecure and confused about what exactly I was asking her to do.

I said it again: "go."

She looked around.

A third time I repeated it: "go!"

The girl said nothing, but began to blush a little. Another child in the group spoke up in an effort to help: "where is she supposed to go?" I wasn't expecting anyone to speak up in the midst of the awkward silence, but that question provided an avenue to explain the central concept of the children's message and, consequently, what this book is about: going where Jesus would have us go, and practicing what Jesus would have us practice.

When the girl sat down, I asked a few of the children if they would hand out peppermints to the entire congregation of over 200 people. This was a large task for only a few of the children to complete and, as it progressed, the inefficiency of the process soon became obvious. If all of the children had helped out, the task would have been completed far more quickly and easily. The purpose of this illustration was to point out that it is not just a few of us who have been called to go, but all of us.

The scriptures are full of "go" stories. In the Old Testament, God sent the Israelites into the Promised Land with a phrase that offered assurance, but commanded trust. However, when a group of spies went to scout out this land of promise, only two of them came back with an enthusiastic, hopeful response: the rest of the group cowered back in fear. Sometimes "go" requires raw faith.

When God's people, the chosen ones, were in Babylon, they probably wouldn't have used the word "sent" to describe their situation. They had been kicked out of their homeland, driven into exile, and displaced into a foreign space. They were strangers brought by God out of the place they knew, out of their familiarity, into Babylon so they could practice exactly what God designed them to be: a demonstration, or a showcase.

This is true in the New Testament as well. People were being sent all over the place, including Jesus himself. The Holy Spirit sent. The disciples sent. Peter, on whom Christ said that he would build his church, addressed a letter to his congregation, scattered through modern-day Turkey. When we are chosen and sent, the church might look more like a diffusion or a spread than a comfortable cluster.

When a person is sent, they will inevitably come back with stories. These stories give faces and names and places to our discoveries. Stories have a way of ingraining themselves in our minds and our hearts. As we respond to being sent, we might come back with a re-definition of miracles or a new kind of faith because something happened that didn't seem possible, or someone said something completely unexpected. The more we "go," the more stories we collect, and the more growth we encounter. Stories and discoveries are important to us and to our faith. They must be personal. We must own them: discipleship cannot happen vicariously.

When I was in grade four, I was late to school one day because of a discovery I made. As I was biking to school, I found a series of hockey cards lying along the newly paved road of a subdivision. This discovery was exciting to me because I collected hockey cards and finding 50 of them on the side of the road seemed amazingly lucky. This scene remains vivid in my memory and I still have those hockey cards today.

I tell this story because it is my story. It is a discovery. It is an event that remains vivid in my memory. I recall details like the rain on the road and on the cards, soaking into these things that seemed to be worthless castoffs, but to me it was all a treasure, and one that I hold close in my heart. It was one of those "I can't believe it" days. It was one of those stories of something I would have never expected and I can never forget the details that composed it.

This story is my story. The key of being sent, of having Jesus say "go" and responding to that commission, is that we gather personal stories to develop our faith. We are not asked to live vicariously through other people's stories, but to grow through our own.

This book assumes that we all love Christ's bride, the church. It has value. It has its place, and covenant theology is a beautiful way to understand the scriptures. However, although we love the church, we are not called to spend our whole lives within its walls. We must move beyond them to fulfill the true purpose of the church and what it is called to be in our world.

I'm here because of covenant theology. I'm here because of the church as an institution, as Christ's bride. I write this book out of a sense of urgency for me, and many others in the church, to be encouraged to put on our shoes, walk out the door, and respond to this word, "go." When we are responsive to "go", it makes the gospel more accessible to all those who pass by the doors of our churches.

This book is also an opportunity for us to work out our faith in fear and trembling. It is a practical book. Call them disciplines. Call them practices. Call them postures. But do not call them programs. Going requires movement and to continue it on like a dance. It has no beginning and no end. There are no questions of "When do we start?" or "When are we done?" because that is not what discipleship is about. One purpose of this book is to shape an understanding about the mercy of God. We know about the forgiveness of God. We know about the love, joy, peace, patience and all of the elements of the Kingdom of God. There are so many, though, who do not know. They have never heard. They have never been shown or taught or introduced to this hope that we live from and stake our lives on. As the church, we are scattered, as Peter writes, because that is a characteristic of those who respond to this word "go." The word 'stranger', too, is a description of who we are in the context of those who live around us: the ones who do not know about the Kingdom of God.

I hope that this book will allow you to taste and see for yourself that the Lord is good and that his Kingdom is coming. I hope it will allow you to discover and experience more "I can't believe it!" days. I hope that you will collect your own stories as opposed to the stories of somebody else, and that you will gather them up like treasure to ponder within your own heart. As your journey takes you further into your neighbourhood, be inspired by the following true stories from the neighbourhoods in our neck of the woods:

THURSDAY, SEPTEMBER 17

WE USED TO HAVE NEIGHBOURS; NOW WE HAVE FRIENDS

"We just spent the last month away in Switzerland (my roots). Our neighbours next door were looking after our home and they did an amazing job. Usually we ask family but it just made more sense to ask our neighbour. Their little 5 year old created a WELCOME HOME sign for us and had it hanging from the bannister. They had 2 freezer meals placed in our freezer! We were so touched. Other neighbours gave us hugs and shared how excited they were to follow our trip on facebook!

I commented to our family: "We used to have neighbours, now we have friends!"

We often say how fortunate we are to live where we do.

One challenge that has been coming up lately is that there is a single mom who moved in this summer with 3 children. She lives with her current boyfriend and his brother. The brokenness is so evident with the children. At first, I was very critical of the kiddos as they have no manners, use bad language, no respect for property, etc etc but lately I've been challenged to love on them so we are aiming to do just that. Not easy but it's our mission."

FRIDAY, AUGUST 21

WHEN YOUR NEIGHBOURS ASK YOU TO DO THE FUNERAL

Over the past year it became clear that our neighbour was in the process of becoming a single parent. Our relationship as neighbours grew slowly and steadily. How it had grown was something I was not aware of until the death of her father earlier this summer. At one point, following the news of her father's death, she asked if I would be willing to do the funeral. You must understand that my role in the community is as a businessman, and, although I am involved as a volunteer leader in our church, I have never been asked to lead a funeral. Having said that, the request to do so was an overwhelming honour. And this made me reflect on how our relationship as ncighbours had progressed over time.

Although the story of our neighbour is filled with tragedy and heartbreak, it was good to know that she felt she could come to us during such circumstances. We are grateful to be there for our neighbour, and we look forward to the continued journey with her.

MONDAY, AUGUST 3

<u>SHOWING UP!</u>

It is amazing how the story line shifts while being present in your neighbourhood.

On Saturday, I ventured over to the gathering of three Thai families who live a few hundred feet away from us, and walked up on to their deck. Here I saw them enjoying sambuka and fried squid (of which I only chose one). The reason I was over there was because earlier we had been discussing the sharing of produce while standing in the communal garden. It was then that I was told two of their children had come over from Thailand and were going to start school this year. "I will introduce them to you tomorrow," he said. When he came the next day, I was not home, and so I proceeded to connect when I saw them on their deck.

After the introduction of their children, I was asked if they could hang around with my kids since they knew no English. It was a an opportunity I didn't see coming from the time we spent in the garden. It just so happens that during the conversation one of women started doing haircuts on the deck. This was an all-too-familiar sight since I grew up in a family that did that too. So, I asked some questions regarding the lady who was cutting hair for her family and in the end found myself getting a haircut as well.

The next day (Sunday) I had a friend ask if we could take the day to sail together. The beauty of where we live is that the lake is nearby. This is also where many of our neighbours live, including one who works and lives in a gated community. She and her husband have been exploring the Scriptures with me over the past month so our relationship is rather new. However, I did know that she gave me the password for the gate that led to a beautiful place to launch our sailing machines. The problem was that the request to come over with friends may be risky, but I decided to phone her anyways in hopes to hear how she would respond. Her response was none other than enthusiastic, and welcomed us with open arms. By the end of the day, our group was 7 in total, but she was so thankful to us for being healthy, positive friends in her life – quite a statement to hear after a few hours of sailing on her secluded beach.

Again, it never ceases to amaze me what can happen when you stand in a garden with a neighbour, walk over to the neighbour's deck for a moment, or make a risky phone call to a new neighbour. These are all open doors that do not need to be walked through. But if we dare venture, we just may find ourselves enjoying how God opens opportunities for us to shine His light.

CHAPTER 1

A Peek from the Balcony

I love maps. Even as a young child, I remember poring over them, looking at them, excited to learn about different places beyond the small world I knew. Today, maps are still an important part of my life. I am a member of an automobile association that gives out maps for free. I am also the father of four and as my children were growing up I thought it would be a great idea, not to mention educational, to go to the auto association and ask them for a map of every country of the world, as well as a whole world map. I brought the maps home in a box and opened it for my kids, who soon began to read over them. They connected places and names that they had heard of before and expanded their repertoire as they encountered new, unfamiliar names and places.

One Christmas, I received a ten pound book that had every map in the world compiled within it. The book is full of detail and every time I open it, I learn something new from its pages. Electronic maps have their place but, to me, they never seem to suffice. I live close to the Rocky Mountains and, during one hiking trip in particular, I credit my map for saving me from an extremely uncomfortable night. My wife and I were looking for the lake where we were going to pitch our tent and became increasingly lost. The marshy ground we trampled through made it impossible to pitch a tent, and as night drew nearer, our water ran out. I turned to the map that I had packed for direction. We finally discovered that we were actually 700 feet above the lake, on a cliff. The map had pointed out our fault and helped us find our destination.

Maps tell a story. They show where you have been, where you are going, and provide guidance when you are lost. Whether it is a paper map, an electronic map, a treasure map, an army map, or the upside down world map: maps ultimately change perspective.

I've been living in the same community for twenty years. I knew many people within it who claimed to be Christians, but eventually I began to wonder what the actual statistics were. What did the concentration of Christians look like within this place that I had lived for years? I began to have conversations with the leadership groups of three fairly large and healthy churches within the area, probing at answers to this question. We talked together about how we could better benefit our communities, but the question of how many Christians were actually spread out in our neighbourhoods remained unanswered.

I decided to use my love of maps to pursue the answer further. I bought a city map, one that divided our span of land into subdivisions and lots, and took this map to the different churches within this community. I went to the Baptist church first, asking the pastor if he would offer the map to his congregation to colour in the places where they lived. Next, I went to the Pentecostal church and asked that congregation to mark where they lived in a different colour. The map then travelled to the Evangelical Free church, the Church of the Nazarene, the Christian Reformed churches, the Lutheran church, and, finally, the local Community Church.

This homemade experiment offered valuable insight, but I knew that it was only a portion of the whole. I knew there were other Christians in the area who hadn't marked their homes, so the map certainly underrepresented the true statistics. However, it began to shape a picture, a glimpse, of how we were spread out in the community. An initial guess projected that there might be about 3% of Christians, of "salt and light" in the community, but the map revealed a 5% representation: and these were just the Christians who attended church. As the map circulated, so did new questions, such as: "Who is that who lives down the street from me?" or "I didn't know there were so many believers on my road!" Some noticed that there were distinct areas of the map with no colour at all. This map ignited discussion as people ran their fingers over the different coloured squares and streets of their community. There was a tangible excitement rising out of this experiment that demanded a sharper vision and direction to move forward.

We needed to clarify who we were to this community and how we could best represent the Kingdom of God in our neighbourhoods.

At this point, the journey became more personal to me. I needed a starting point. I gathered some of the Christians that lived close to me, within an area of about 100 houses and invited them over for coffee and dessert at my house. While they were there, I asked them if they could draw a map of their neighbourhood. Of course, we all lived in roughly the same neighbourhood, but I'd heard once that everyone has a different idea of what their neighbourhood looks like. This proved to be true. One person drew a map of the neighbourhood that was spread far beyond the 100 houses that I had in mind. Some drew maps of only a handful of houses. As the evening and discussion progressed, we sketched out an average boundary of our community and tried to name the people in those houses. If we couldn't name them, we tried to describe who they were, like: "the one with the big dogs," or "the grumpy lady" or "the old man" or "the house with renters in it."

We wrote these names and descriptions on our map and, throughout the night we began to wonder if we had been missing something key about the scriptures' command to love our neighbours. We realized that we were simply existing beside, or driving by, these people who lived right next door to us without thinking about how to love them.

A few years earlier, my wife and I used to regularly walk through our neighbourhood block, often meeting other walkers along the way. It was around this time that I started to think seriously about how we could love the neighbours that lived around us, the ones that I had simply driven past for about 15 years at that point. It had recently come to my attention that there had been a death in our community and, although I didn't know who the person really was, I decided to attend the funeral. As I watched pictures flashing up on the screen, I realized that this was a woman that my wife and I had walked past so many times, but had never stopped to say anything, except maybe the odd "hello." She had a rare condition and when she was admitted to the hospital, her body turned septic and, within a few hours, she died. She was only in her early 40's. I felt like I had a connection with her since I had walked past her on a regular basis, yet I had never taken advantage of any opportunities to truly interact with her.

These maps we had been drawing up began to reveal a new picture of who lived in my community, where they lived, and how they lived. More importantly, they began to develop a vision that not only showed us how much salt and light already existed in our neighbourhood, but also all the people who needed this salt and who needed to see our light. Be encouraged by the maps, but be more encouraged by the true stories that make these maps come to life:

SUNDAY, JULY 12

MARRIAGE RENEWAL IN THE NEIGHBOURHOOD

This past weekend my wife and I celebrated with two of our neighbours as they renewed their vows. Evan & Shannon had separated for a lengthy period of time, but did not want to be part of a "throw-away culture." Therefore, they renewed their vows.

There was nothing you could say was legally binding about the night, but the dress code and formalities would have made anyone believe this was a *real* wedding. It was refreshing because this all came from 25 years of marriage experience. Therefore, the beauty came from the intentional act of being like Christ....giving ourselves to the other as Christ did for the church, and as the church then submitted to Christ (Ephesians 5). There was nothing easy here, but the depth of joy and the demonstration of faithfulness has been enriching for us all.

Thank you, Evan & Shannon, for giving me permission to share this story of renewal.

Thank you for walking alongside each other in search for a deeper life with Christ, and allowing me to be part of that journey. And I look forward to more conversations about God, life and how we can journey together.

SATURDAY, JUNE 27

NEW KID ON THE BLOCK

The guy was tattooed and had guns of steel! I had seen him walk by the house almost daily, even engaging in small talk as the kids and I played in the front yard. My son found him muscular, my daughter didn't like all the tattoos and I wasn't sure what to think. I did wonder where he belonged in the neighbourhood. Time came for our annual block party, where all those on our street gather to celebrate, have bike parades, play games, reconnect and cultivate new friendships. As I walked down the street with another neighbour, collecting signatures for the block party, she asked if I had seen the 'new guy'. I immediately knew who she was referring to because he had quite the presence about him! She found him scary and wasn't sure what to think. Interestingly, about 5 minutes later he was walking behind us on the street. Through a tight grin, my friend informed me of his presence. Wanting to break down a few boundaries, I turned around and introduced myself and explained a bit about our upcoming block party. My friend was in absolute shock at my boldness, but 'Mr. Tattoo' was quite interested in the block party. He was given an invite and even offered his services. Apparently he works in the adult entertainment business! We politely mentioned the family focus of this event. All was well, and we left the conversation with a smile and a new connection.

TUESDAY, JUNE 9

WITH OR WITHOUT GOD

Last week I met a man who told me, "I believe in God today because of my neighbour." He continued to tell me the story about his ongoing relationship with this neighbour, who obviously put his love for God and neighbour at the forefront.

During these months of block parties and community garage sales, I often ask people what they are planning for the next event that could not be accomplished without God's intervention. The question allows us to think less about logistics and the numbers, and more about these events as vehicles we can use to see what God is up to in our neighbourhoods. Here we begin to redeem the purpose and value of such events.

The Bible is filled with stories of accomplishments that were achieved only as God's people sought, accepted and invested power from beyond themselves: God's power to achieve their God-honoured goals. Far too often we try to do too much on our own, forgetting that there is help available from the One who made us, loves us, and walks with us in all of life's experiences.

May our love for a neighbour and for God always be on the front page of the instruction book we are following.

TUESDAY, JUNE 9

<u>ELLEN</u>

Our neighbours just picked up their FLEX car from our local Ford dealer last night. They won it on the Ellen show so there was a lot of buzz about that. You've probably heard the story too. It's a fun one. They drove into the close last night honking their horns with both the old and new vehicle. Some of us went out to check it out and others waved from their doorsteps.

CHAPTER 2

Windsurfing, Money and Health

A few years ago, I attended a conference with over 200 church planters. At the beginning of our seminar, the speaker asked us to raise our hands if we had been discipled at some point in our lives. Of all the 200 people, only five hands raised. The speaker then asked how many of us had discipled another person. Only three hands stayed up.

Some people may have been discipled without even knowing it fit under the term "discipleship," but, regardless, an uncomfortably small number of people had responded to these questions. This was a room filled with people who wanted to lead and guide in a way that would bring new life into their communities, but only five people had really experienced some form of discipleship. This was concerning, although it did not completely surprise me at the time. In our North American culture, discipline is not always promoted or encouraged. It can be difficult to sustain.

When I was a teenager, I would drive to a lake near my house to watch the windsurfers cut across the water at high speeds. One day, two old men caught my attention as they assembled their windsurfing gear. When I approached them and asked them their ages, I found out that they were 70 and 72, respectively. They then launched onto their windsurfing boards, letting the wind do all the work, and effortlessly glided across the lake at a breathtaking speed, especially for two 70-year-old men. They returned shortly after to take a break, and I took advantage of the opportunity to ask them how they had become so adept at this sport. One of the old men replied, with wisdom that comes from experience, "if you practice the disciplines of windsurfing, you make the wind do all the work for you. It becomes natural and easy to do, even at our age."

After this encounter, I became inspired to take up windsurfing myself. I wanted to understand what that man meant and how people could still windsurf at the age of 70 and 72. Windsurfing is somewhat of a dying sport today, and part of the reason why it is losing popularity is because of the initial disciplines that must be mastered. The art of windsurfing requires balance and learning how to gain speed and momentum with the wind. It demands trust in your equipment and trust in the wind, which often blows inconsistently. It is important to learn how to master steering, as well. It is easy to lose "ground" by coasting with the wind, and getting back to where you started requires technique. The principle of windsurfing is not simply to go downwind, but to go across it. In fact, with the proper equipment, you can actually go upwind. The construction of the sail allows the wind not only to fill it, but also to work around it. This creates lift, which creates speed, which allows you to turn upwind. The fin underneath the board pushes against the water, forcing it around it, which also creates lift. This provides maneuverability and enables the windsurfer to go up against the wind.

Aside from the balance, the speed, the trust, and the steering, there are two technical terms that I learned when I first began to windsurf. On my first day of windsurfing class we learned about the center of lateral resistance and the center of effort. Both of these concepts were central to learning the basic technique of windsurfing, but as I sat on the beach, listening to the instructor, I was just anxious to get onto the water. I wondered how essential these terms actually were. Maybe we could just learn them later, I thought. When I finally got onto the board, though, I immediately realized that all the preparation we had just undergone on the beach was a critical foundation. We needed to understand the basics and the technicalities of this sport in order to understand how to move with the sail and work with the wind. Over the years, I've come to master the disciplines of balance and speed and trust and steering. I can now plane across the water like those 70-year-old men who had initially inspired me to explore their sport.

Often, the reason it is so difficult to learn or achieve something beautiful is the time commitment and effort involved. However, investing this time and effort can lead to great reward. When I go windsurfing, the silence and the speed shapes a space of worship for me. Learning to master discipline often provides an avenue toward deeper experiences and lasting change.

There was a point in my life, many years after learning to windsurf, when I realized that I was gaining a little too much weight. I decided to enter a contest at a local college called "Fit and Firm," which began a journey for me in a new form of discipline in health. During the course of the contest, which took place from October to December, I lost 40 pounds.

Transformation definitely occurred over those three months, yet it was hard for me to tell until I looked at the before and after pictures of myself. Of course, there was evidence along the way of needing smaller sizes of clothing, but I couldn't see the dramatic change until I compared those old pictures to the new ones. The contest taught me about the hard work of discipline and the transformation it leads to. Losing 40 pounds was hard overall, but the disciplines that I learned to implement made some parts of the journey easier. I learned them as a set of practices. They were practices of overcoming temptation, of creating a daily rhythm, and of forming new habits.

One principle that I had to learn was that the process of losing weight is not just about restrictive eating. I checked in at the halfway point of the contest and discovered that I had already lost 23 of those 40 pounds. This seemed like great progress, but the instructor who was measuring me for the contest had a different perspective. He said that, yes, I had lost 23 pounds, but they might not have been the kind of pounds I wanted to lose. He lectured me about increasing muscle mass instead of just losing pounds. He told me that there are healthy transformations and unhealthy transformations, and that I needed to pay attention to muscle increase. During the second half of the competition, I altered some of my rhythms and practices in order to gain muscle instead. That is how I won second place in the competition and got the prize money I had been working for. The man who won first place was very deserving of it, as he had obviously become quite muscular over the course of these four months. He understood what my trainer had told me at the halfway point: the discipline of becoming healthy is a practice of gaining life instead of draining it away.

21

Another area in my life that I have learned the value of discipline is in the realm of finances. Over time, discipline also helped me save money. The point isn't the dollar amount as much as the practices I learned to implement in order to gain that money.

My wife and I met with a financial consultant and read a few books that he recommended. Then, we began to build some of the practices into our lives. It wasn't just a conversation or an idea; it was an alteration in our lifestyle. It was a slow change that carried on. Often, whether it is with windsurfing, a "Fit and Firm" competition, or with our finances, we wait for inspiration or a conversation or a meeting before we start to implement the discipline into our lives. With our finances, we took our actual money, divided it into piles according to budget items, and used only the money that was allocated to each budget in our spending. As we fell into this rhythm and pattern of thinking, we began to straighten out our finances and found the ability to save considerably more money than we used to. My wife and I had both experienced a frugal upbringing, which helped, and the financial consultant was there to guide us, and we took classes teaching us that we had to tell our money where to go, rather than letting it slip through our fingers and wondering where it went. However, the disciplines we learned to apply transformed our lives.

In the scriptures, the gospels of Matthew, Mark, Luke and John, present stories of people taking hold of practices and disciplines in their lives. This is the church and how it grows. The church is comprised of individuals on a journey of growth through learning and applying life-giving practices. There is a massive body of people walking the path of transformation. The word "church," then, can be thought of as a byproduct of what happens as a result of these practices. It is a community of people learning together how to live. Discipleship is difficult, though. In the scriptures, some of the disciples turned away because they felt that the discipline was too hard for them. It wasn't appealing. This might not be far off from the feelings we have as we try to lose weight, or build muscle mass, or master windsurfing, or get our finances in order.

Yet we are drawn back into our neighbourhoods when we see God at work such as we see in the following true stories from our local neighbourhoods:

FRIDAY, MAY 15

NEIGHBOURHOOD TEARS

I'd known her for some time, but had not really connected on a personal level. Defining our relationship as acquaintances would be accurate. We spoke often, shared friends but it was still quite superficial. Last fall, something inside inspired me to deepen this relationship and so I trusted the prompting of the Holy Spirit, stepped out of my comfort zone and invited her and two other neighbours for a weekend away. Just the ladies… it sounded divine. In fact, it was divine as God allowed for a deepening of those relationships in a way I could have never expected. We are now fast friends, sharing and depending on each other as family. She shared of some significant challenges her husband was facing in his work. They were worried and the stress was bringing him to an unhealthy place. One week in particular, they kept coming to my mind; the Holy Spirit again. I had been praying for them on my own, but hadn't necessarily shared that with them. They are not believers, so I was trying to be respectful. Finally, I sent a text, telling them they were on my heart and asking for their permission to pray for them as a couple, their family and the challenges happening at his work. She responded with a text, explaining that my message had brought her husband to tears. His comment was "who needs family when you live in a neighbourhood like this". Praise God for what he is doing in our hood. I am privileged and honoured to come alongside His plans for our street.

TUESDAY, APRIL 21

<u>WHERE CONVERSATIONS LEAD</u>

A simple story: My need for a ride to the airport left me wondering from whom in my church I could get a ride. Not long after, my neighbour met me outside and asked how I was getting to the airport for my trip (since he already knew from earlier conversations). I told him that I did not know yet. His next response was filled with curiosity when he asked why I had not thought of him. Of course, the idea of leaving at 5 am for the airport seems to limit your options to a select group of drivers. But he reminded me that he was always up at that time….and proceeded to remind me that I knew this fact.

This led to an invitation to have him over for supper. As we prepared to sit down for a meal, I led a prayer as is the custom in our household. This was not so for him and his household. In addition to giving thanks for the gift of food, I prayed for his three children, by name. Following the prayer, I noticed him subtly wiping away a couple of tears as he re-positioned his chair and regained his composure.

Simple opportunities can sometimes be easily overlooked when we could be naturally loving our neighbours.

MONDAY, MARCH 30

INTENTIONAL MOVE

After 17 years in Calgary we never actually felt at home there. My husband and I are perhaps a bit nomadic, so we were more than ready for a change. Despite making plenty of money there, it just wasn't great. We left our jobs and family and started looking around. Not for work but for a place to call home; a community of people who cared about each other, that we could contribute to and feel a part of. Enter Laurier Heights. 8 months in and our lives are transformed. Work will be work pretty much wherever, but home is resoundingly right where we have landed. This is partly because of the Abundant Community initiative coming to us and partly because we are venturing out of our way to connect.

I could go on and on about how much differently we look at the world now. We have begun to really value our little trade-economy we have with neighbours – even in something simple like babysitting. Our lives are enriched by the visits we have with the people we have met and the ways in which those relationships are being sustained.

Chapter 3

The Agenda

There is a story I often tell about a businessman who once approached his pastor and said: "Pastor, you preached a great message this morning about finances and tithing our resources, but I have a question for you. I'm a businessman. Is my 10% tithe off of net or gross?"

The pastor replied: "Sir, when you get close to giving 10%, come back and ask me that question again."

The businessman's question reveals his heart. He was missing the point of the discipline of tithing because his priorities were all wrong. The pastor knew that if the businessman actually started tithing and working the practice into his life, his initial question would have become irrelevant. His paradigm would have shifted.

Disciplines are difficult to implement, but they do have a way of changing our perspective. Disciplines expand our vision and reveal things that we may have previously overlooked. When people talk to me about the adventure of practically loving their neighbours, they often question where it will lead them. It is difficult to answer that kind of question on the outset of the journey. Learning to embrace this discipline will inevitably reveal something new to every person. Each story will be unique because we all enter in with our own past, our own experiences, and we engage with different people. The discipline of loving our neighbour shapes us all differently.

When my mom and dad retired, they wanted to build a new home. In the process of planning and designing it, they decided to place the patio, on which they hoped to have coffee on a regular basis, at the front of the house facing the sidewalk. This was an intentional choice. Most people place their patios at the back of the home and use it as a space of retreat. However, my mom said that they wanted to have the patio out front so they could engage with their neighbourhood, rather than hide away from it.

This "front porch" mentality, an idea that was more common in the 1940's, 50's and 60's, was a way for my parents to connect and listen and practice the discipline of loving the neighbours around them. They found that many people wanted to talk about their celebrations and their trials in life. Most people wanted someone to listen and to acknowledge them. Out of this willingness to be present, my parents began to receive invitations from their neighbours and, as a result, gained new opportunities to participate in the lives of the people in their community.

When my mom told me this story, I was reminded that the discipline of loving our neighbours requires intentionality and thought. It is easy to stay wrapped up in our own lives. However, stepping out and welcoming others alongside us enriches the journey in ways that we can hardly anticipate at the outset. For my parents, simply choosing to sit on the front porch and actively take an interest in the lives of others allowed them to build relationships and seize opportunities that may have otherwise been missed.

Sometimes people ask me if I have an "agenda" when it comes to loving my neighbour. What they are really wondering, here, is how to approach this discipline. I say that it starts in your heart. Your agenda is really your motivation. *Why* do you want to love your neighbour? Listening to your neighbour because you genuinely want to build a relationship with them looks different from listening to your neighbour because you want them to go to church or come to a program with you. Knowing your own motivation requires personal reflection and discernment. This is important to understand.

For those of us who grew up in church, the idea of loving your neighbour can quickly twist itself into evangelistic tactics. In the church, when we talk about loving our neighbours, it can sometimes seem synonymous to the idea of "getting your neighbour to church" or converting them. This is a mentality that leads to guilt, though. We might worry that we said the wrong thing or that because our neighbour isn't coming to church, we are somehow failing as witnesses. The truth is that love isn't a script and it certainly isn't a way to manipulate others into going to church.

We aren't called to love our neighbours out of duty. I know that my upbringing instilled a strong work ethic within me. I learned that there are things you have to do because they are necessary, whether or not you feel like doing them. This mentality commonly crosses into our view of evangelism and the Scriptures as well. We can view it, as a friend once told me, as the "top-down" approach: it has been legislated, therefore, we must do it. This, again, circles around to the question of motivation. Why are you really trying to love your neighbour? Is it fuelled by fear or obligation? Is it because you "should" or because you feel genuinely compelled to?

While trying to navigate these questions of motivation and duty, I personally came to an understanding that loving your neighbour is best practiced within the mindset of "tasting" the Kingdom of Heaven. The motivation, the fuel, should stem from the unconditional love we experience in Jesus Christ. This is what ignites our passion and drives us to love others, too. It is clear in the scriptures that God is a forgiving God. He is slow to anger and merciful. He is abundant in grace. If God's love was conditional, we would not be able to experience the true freedom and celebration of life. Of course there is deep pain and suffering in our world. There is a great deal to mourn. However, the unconditional love of Christ can spur us forward. It can be our anchor. It can be the motivation for us to share this unconditional love with others and allow them to experience a taste of the Kingdom as well, by offering grace, and maybe a listening ear.

I won't pretend that this is always an easy thing to do. Unconditional love doesn't come naturally to us. It is rare and not often extended to us in our human experience. We all love imperfectly at times, usually with conditions. The only true example of unconditional love we have on a human level is that of Jesus Christ. We won't be able to love our neighbours perfectly in every situation, but the important part, the grace, is knowing that the unconditional love of Jesus is our motivation. We are not fuelled by our own agendas or tallying the amount of people we have witnessed to. We are searching for what God might be already doing in our communities and prayerfully considering our role in the story. We are joining God in his greater plan, as opposed to making our own personal agenda and asking him to bless it. Our drive should come from seeking a further taste of the Kingdom of God through unconditional love.

At first, loving my neighbour was a task that felt more like a chore. It was very unnatural for me. After a period of time of intentionally making myself available, though, I found that God revealed himself in surprising ways. God would peel back the surface of the situation and show me where he was at work. It motivated me to action as I began to see and hear God in tangible ways. Sometimes, at night, I would think over what I had experienced that day and say things like *I can't believe that happened!* It increased my awareness of God and redefined my understanding of the word "miracle."

It was these tastes of the Kingdom of God that prompted me to continue the practice of loving my neighbour. I didn't do it out of obligation. I did it because I wanted to see and experience more of the surprises that God had in store; the ones I couldn't see beyond my own agenda. I was curious and inspired to see more of what God could do in me and through me as I explored this journey of loving my neighbour.

All of life belongs to God. This truth runs straight through the Bible from Genesis to Revelation. As we continue to make ourselves available, there are two areas where we can see God at work. The first area is within brokenness. The second is within beauty. I believe that these are two simple ideas that can offer direction in our search to see and hear God at work. When we are proactive in loving our neighbours, applying the disciplines, gaining a sense of personal direction, and shaping the story of our neighbourhoods, we can intentionally capture opportunities to be used by God. There are active and passive ways to approach this.

Around 8:00 one Sunday morning in June, I was setting up a sign for our neighbourhood block party. I had started a habit of walking up and down the streets of my neighbourhood, listening and watching for where God might be at work, but nothing had become very clear to me yet. This morning, though, I noticed one of my neighbours, named Jack, in his yard. I knew that he and his young wife were truckers by trade and that they usually woke up early, around 4:00 in the morning. On the days that they didn't have to get up early, they slept very late. He had told me a little about his rhythm of life, emphasizing how busy they were.

On this particular Sunday morning, Jack was out trimming the bushes in his yard. I was thinking about the rest of my morning. I knew I had to go to church in a few hours. I wanted coffee and some time to be quiet before that. I wanted to be available to my children. Suddenly, all of these things seemed very pressing and crowded in my head as I stood there, aware that Jack was trimming his bushes down the street. The fact that Jack was at home and awake at this time was highly irregular, and for him to be trimming his bushes at this time was even more rare. I could not ignore the distinct tug in my heart to go over and talk with him.

I fought back in my mind. My entire goal in going outside was to set up the block party. That was neighbouring too, wasn't it? I knew I was making excuses. I decided to listen to the prompting, divert from my morning plans, and walk the 400 meters down the street to talk to Jack.

Jack stopped trimming long enough to say "hello." At first we engaged in a bit of small talk, but I immediately noticed that something was wrong. Something was off: I could see it in his face. There were tears in his eyes.

"What's going on?" I asked sincerely. I didn't know that God would use this simple question so profoundly.

Jack began to open up to me, revealing that he had just returned from the other side of the country where they had held a celebration of his mother's life. Sadly, she had died young. A year before, she had been diagnosed with a cancer that quickly became aggressive and, eventually, led to her death. I simply stood and listened to Jack pour out his story. He clearly wanted to tell it. He needed someone to listen as he navigated this profound grief over a mother who died too young. He said it was unfair. He told me how beautiful she was and how she always had good intentions. He told me about all of the things she had still wanted to accomplish. The conversation did become lengthy but, although I was very aware that I needed to go to church, I also knew that God often reveals himself through interruptions to our daily routine. Jack needed me to listen in this moment and I needed to be present with him.

This is a passive way in which I experienced God revealing himself through engaging in the brokenness of my neighbour's life. The moment presented itself to me. I didn't seek it out. However, we can also be more active in pursuing these moments where we might gain a taste of the Kingdom and experience God's work in the brokenness around us.

I'm thinking about Alex. My wife and I knew Alex and his wife because we would cross paths at sports tournaments and, sometimes, we would take time to hang out and drink beer together, or we'd share tools from our garages. One day, as we were preparing for a garage sale weekend, I began to initiate a conversation. I want to emphasize that this wasn't on my "agenda," but it stemmed out of a desire to uncover where God might be at work in this relationship.

I asked Alex one simple question: "Do you ever get angry?" This question wasn't random, and Alex wasn't surprised that I asked it. We had already built up a certain relational equity between us and I already knew that the answer would be "yes," even before it left his lips. I was going somewhere with this. Again, this was not because I needed to check another box in my list of "to do" regarding this friend, or because I wanted to manipulate him into something. I wasn't overthinking this. Instead, I wanted to explore who Alex was as a person. I cared about him, and I was hoping to guide the relationship into deeper territory.

Before Alex said anything else, I said that I struggled with anger, myself. I told him a story about how I treated our dog because I had a bad day at work. I said that I had a tendency to become frustrated under certain kinds of circumstances. I said that I knew I had no good justification for my behaviour, but I did realize that it was an issue within me that I needed to deal with.

My vulnerability in that moment gave Alex permission to open up with me. He began to share and expose new parts of his own story. I started to gain a clearer picture of where he had come from and how he was being shaped. I could gauge where he was at in his life, where God's fingerprints were showing up, and where I could possibly encourage or direct Alex in the midst of it.

These are examples of how we can be alert to God amidst the hard and broken areas of life. However, God not only meets us and teaches us through brokenness, but he also reveals himself in areas of beauty. Here are a few more true neighbourhood stories that highlight this fact:

MONDAY, FEBRUARY 23

FRONT STEP TEAR DROPS

The other night, I was woken by the sound of crying. Standing in sleepy disorientation I couldn't quite figure out where it was coming from, but I knew it was close. I looked out my windows, and peeped out the little glass panes on my door, but I could see nothing. I was about to go back to bed but heard it once more. I woke up my husband, and when he opened the door to take a look, we discovered a neighbour and her daughter sitting on our front step, crying and cold. I will spare the details of the long night, other than to say that as I sat with this woman, and my husband sat with her husband back at their home, the stories of pain, loss, hopelessness, shame, anger and sadness were absolutely heart wrenching.

Living and loving in the community you reside is messy business. It's hard, it hurts, it costs. It might not end the way we hope. It's uncomfortable sometimes. There is beauty, undoubtedly, but there is also a great deal of pain.

In the course of our conversation, the young woman shared that this is not the first time she had sat on our front steps in the night. She needed help, and wanted help, but knocking on the door was just too painful, fearful and shameful for her. Still, she came and sat on our steps.

Likely, it is not common that we will have a neighbour finding refuge on our physical front steps, but we do have entire communities who are sitting on our front steps in other ways. We live with many who need help, and want help, and can't find their way to knock. I am left wondering how I might open the door and invite Jesus to wipe the tears on the front steps of my neighbourhood.

MONDAY, FEBRUARY 2

<u>T</u>HREE YEARS INTO A NEW NEIGHBOURHOOD

We moved to Peachland, BC: a relatively small community of just over 5000; mostly retired people. We left Abbotsford, BC where I facilitated a home group to have a new direction in our lives here in the Okanagan Valley.

I was asking God what he wanted me to do here in our new neighbourhood. The strong answer I received was 'Love your neighbour's'. Since then, we have been intentional to connect with neighbours on our street.

From shoveling snow to assisting a neighbour with their rockwork, to watching houses and gardens for neighbours away for short periods, to making up a part for another neighbours quad to using my pickup and shovels to pick up horse manure for neighbours garden beds or for doing shared dump runs. We have been moving towards building relationships in our neighbourhood.

Yet at the same time, I am being taught by non- church-goer neighbours that as Christians, we don't necessarily have a corner on the market towards being good neighbours.

Pockets of our neighbourhood are already connecting by sharing an annual progressive dinner or potluck which we have been included with for the last 3 summers since we moved here. A close neighbour is sharing her raised garden beds with other neighbours as she can't keep up with them at this point.

Recently I decided to make up a contact list for our neighbourhood. It includes addresses, peoples' names, telephone numbers, email addresses and emergency contact (if they would like to include that info). Most neighbours by far are happy to join the list while a small few would prefer to be left out as they seem to be valuing their privacy, which I am happy to do – after making some personal notes about the encounter. You see, we get the odd bear that wanders through peoples' yards: a great reason to share contact info for quick email or phone contacts to put out a warning!

While calling or visiting neighbours, I have identified a fair group of those who would like to connect, which I see as the fertile ground.

Comments such as 'Are you calling to invite me to a party?' have been fun to engage with and show that there is true openness to taking things further in building relationships. I look forward to hosting an event or just being available to those I can sense are responsive. I will up my neighbourhood walks as the weather improves to pray for our neighbourhood as well as be available to connect with others outside.

There are real bonuses already happening. I was invited in yesterday to see a new litter of puppies and was able to explain at that time that their neighbour with 'the loud Harley Davidson' was actually a really nice guy with a young family who offered to help with whatever I need mechanically yet has a disability that keeps him out of work.

Building bridges. First fruits...

Part Two

Storytime

There's a game we used to play with the youth I've pastored over the years. It involves three teams and each team gets a tractor pulling a wagon of hay bales. This game usually takes places in the winter when there is a few inches of snow on the ground. The point of the game is to get as many hay bales on your team's wagon as possible by stealing bales off of the other team's wagons as the tractors drive slowly around the field.

The interesting thing about this game is that sometimes the goal of maintaining the most bales becomes secondary to fights over individual bales. The competition can get intense. Often two youths will battle for one hay bale while the tractors move on. That one bale will be torn apart by the end of the fight and everyone else will be far ahead, still engaged in the competition, but, for some fascinating reason, that one hay bale becomes a kind of prize that neither youth is willing to give up. Even when the bale falls apart, they will still continue to tackle each other for the bits and pieces of hay. At some point, when the bale is completely torn apart, they look up and realize the futility of what they have been fighting for. The hay bale has no value, especially when it is broken apart and scattered across the ground. The wagons have left them behind, and they usually have to run a far distance to catch up.

I see a metaphor, here. In the context of church, I've observed a tendency for some of us to become so wrapped up in certain elements of the organization and the programs that we miss the objective of actually engaging with the world we are called to serve. It moves on, like the wagons, while we are still tussling over hay bales. If we take a step back, maybe it would expand our perspective and shift our priorities. As we continue to explore the concept of neighbouring in this book, I want to emphasize practices over programs. Practices offer direction, yet allow room to breathe and create and allow our relationships to grow in their own unique ways. We're ripping a page from the disciple's book to move us forward into mission. The point is less about what the structures and the organizations of church look like, and more about how we are fulfilling the reason for them. I realize that this does raise a certain tension. Meetings and programs, although good, are something we've linked so intimately to church, but sometimes the planning and schedules can choke out the time and the energy that could be otherwise redirected to invest in practically living out our mission.

I was speaking to a young adult, once, who simply asked me when he would get another opportunity to serve in the church. This simple question snapped my vision into focus. I realized that I should be placing more energy into shaping practices in my life, rather than perfecting programs.

If you and I were sitting down for coffee and we were talking about how to fulfill this calling to love our neighbours, I can guarantee that you would mention one of two things, or both, in connection to living out this practice: busyness and fear. I want to address this briefly before we move on.

Our culture knows busyness well. It is real, and we all know the pressure of a bursting schedule or wishing for extra hours in the day. How, then, do we squeeze in time to love our neighbours in addition to the energy we invest into making our regular lives function? My answer is to change your perspective from doing "for" your neighbour to doing "with" your neighbour. Rather than making them a project, take them alongside you. Invite them into what you are already doing, rather than adding them to your list of "to-do."

To address the issue of fear: it is repeated over and over in the scriptures "do not fear." We are commanded not to fear. However, humanly speaking, we all wrestle with fear, especially in the area of making new connections with people. This is mostly because many of us are somewhat out of practice in the area of loving our neighbours. The solution to this is simply to move forward, start practicing, and get back into shape so that we can return back to the field strong and effective and relevant in our play.

Roof Project Healing

The neighbourhood that we live in consists of about 40 homes and a diverse mix of people. They come from a range of different faith and non-faith backgrounds, all ages are represented, some people are in their second or third marriage, some families have children, and they all have very different occupations and time schedules. This is the anatomy of our community, which probably isn't so different from your neighbourhood. Connections are often made through children who play together or people who are willing to share things and this is an amazing example of how we can live out practices, rather than programs, in our lives. Again, we are not focusing on developing programs that start and end at specific times, but we are trying to knead intentionality, or a kind of alertness, into our lives that makes serving and loving people a natural life rhythm.

In my neighbourhood, one particular home used to stand out because it was obviously not being cared for properly. Joe, the man who owned the house, had four young children with his wife when she left him suddenly. This left him trying to maintain working at his job and raising four children on his own. As he tried to juggle all of this, maintaining his house and yard fell lower on his list of priorities. Joe didn't tell anyone that his wife had left him, but others in the community began to wonder if something was wrong, since the yard, which had been previously well kept, continued to look worse.

Somehow the story surfaced that Joe's wife had left and that he was trying to manage his life alone. Four other neighbours and I decided to gather together and brainstorm different ways we could possibly help Joe and alleviate some of the pressure in his life. One person pointed out that his roof needed repair and that we could probably gather a group of people to help fix it as a way to bless Joe. This idea got the most traction and soon we had rallied a group of people who were excited about the project.

We thought that the hardest part of the whole project, ironically, would be actually asking Joe if we could use our gifts to help him fix his roof. We thought it might hurt his pride a bit, even though we didn't want to make it seem like we were helping him out of pity. We shouldn't have worried. One of the people in our group volunteered to go over and graciously present our idea to Joe. He returned a mere 20 minutes later with the news that Joe had agreed to accept our help.

In September, we stripped the roof down and put everything in order to do the actual work on the following day. We had about 20 neighbours helping out. Some were on the roof and others, who were afraid of heights, worked on painting Joe's window frames. A few mothers got the idea to fill Joe's freezer with food and pre-made meals for he and his children to enjoy. Joe was right there with us. It was, admittedly, a little overwhelming for him, but the whole event had a celebratory feel to it and was done very tastefully. We did not want to make Joe feel like a charity case, but rather to empower him by showing support.

While we were working on the house, a car pulled into the driveway. A middle aged couple came out, apparently very interested in what we were doing. I climbed off of the roof and approached them. I knew they couldn't be from our neighbourhood because I didn't recognize them at all. I greeted them and soon discovered that the couple were actually Joe's parents. This surprised me. I asked them where they were from.

"Regina" they said. Regina was nine hours away from Joe's house.

"Oh, you've come to visit your son?" I asked.

"Not exactly" they said. "We heard from Joe what was going on in this neighbourhood and we couldn't believe it. We got into our car early this morning and drove all the way so we could see it for ourselves."

"So the only reason you are here," I clarified, "is because your son told you that we were fixing his roof? You drove nine hours straight here so that you could witness this yourself?"

"Yes!" they said. There were tears in Joe's mother's eyes as she looked at the people on the roof, joking and laughing, with Joe right in the middle of it all.

Later, when the roof was finished, we all sat around the fire outside at Joe's place with a few drinks. We listened to the parents talk about Joe's hard story and how grateful they were that this community was rallying to support him. They said that they had been telling Joe to move to a different area, to get away from this place, but now they were glad he had stayed where he was.

This was not the only beautiful story to emerge from that day. As we were all saying good night and preparing to leave, a woman came up to me and said "Rick, this was great. Especially with Tom and Henry!"

"Who?" I asked.

"Tom and Henry, wasn't that amazing?"

"I don't know. I mean, I guess. I was expecting them to come," I said.

"No, you don't know about Tom and Henry?" she said "This turned out so beautifully."

"The roof?" I ventured.

"No- Tom and Henry on the roof" she said. She told me that Tom and Henry had lived beside each other for five years and they had not been friendly neighbours. They had done things to each other that had caused both deep regret and painful memories. The fact that Tom and Henry could set aside their differences to collaborate in creating something beautiful for Joe was further evidence of God's hand at work in this story.

When I heard this, tears came to my eyes. I had been dangerously close to patting myself on the back for organizing this project, especially since it had gone so well. The Tom and Henry story humbled me, though. It reminded me that there was so much more going on than what I could control or plan for. I had simply been obedient, but God did the real work of transformation.

Today, I sometimes receive texts from neighbours telling me that they saw Tom and Henry wave at each other on their way to work in the morning, or that they were seen talking together and sharing things. These are all pure signs of the healing that is happening in their relationship.

As we begin to actively obey and implement these practices, or ways of being, in our lives, we can expect these kind of surprises and stories to surface.

THE PRACTICE OF REIMAGINING

The first practice I want us to explore is that of reimagining our neighbourhoods. What I mean by this is training ourselves to see our community in a different way and remaining open to new potential in our activities and in our relationships. I have a friend who says, sometimes, that "we do not know what we do not know," and I want to acknowledge from the beginning that this is possibly the largest barrier we will encounter as we implement the practice of reimagining. Changing our mindset and the way we see our neighbourhoods can be difficult at first, especially when we are not sure what we are supposed to be seeing differently.

We do not know what we do not know.

Perhaps a few stories will help explain this concept more clearly.

One gorgeous day in the summer of 2014, I went to a neighbour's house to watch the semi-final game of World Cup soccer: the highly anticipated match between Germany and Brazil. At this point, I had been invested in my community for a number of years and I was aware that one neighbour, an eighty-year-old German man named Doug who lived alone in his home, was a huge fan of the German soccer team. I had seen him wearing German fan paraphernalia and he made it clear that he was proud to be cheering for "his" team.

The game began with an unbelievable string of goals that secured Germany's 5-0 lead by half time. I realized, at this point, that Doug would absolutely be watching this game and that it would probably be very safe for me to stop by. His team was winning by a healthy margin, so I knew that if I showed up, I wouldn't be distracting him in a tense moment. I also assumed that he would be in a particularly good mood on this day of all days.

As I made my way over to his house, I spent some time thinking and praying about what might happen when I got there. In reality, I had no reason to worry. Doug was overjoyed that his team was winning and, when he saw me coming, he flew out of his house to give me a giant hug. He invited me inside and offered me something to drink. All I had to do was practice being present. My only job was to sit and watch the soccer game with this gentleman.

As the game wore on, the gap in the score continued to widen to 7-0. Suddenly, quite abruptly, Doug invited me to come see something downstairs. I was surprised. Doug was a huge Germany fan, and even though his team was clearly winning, I would have expected him to be riveted on the game the whole time. He seemed distracted by something else, though.

I'm always willing to explore open doors and see where God might be leading, so I followed Doug down the basement stairs with the soccer game blaring in the background. Doug searched for the lights and, as he flicked them on, I tried to get a sense of the room in the dim lighting. I saw a pool table in the middle of the floor, but that wasn't what Doug wanted me to see. He screwed in another light bulb and flicked another switch to shed more light in the dark space.

The basement was like a little shrine. The walls were covered in awards. Doug went over and touched a few of them proudly, while pointing out more with his other hand as he told me about his teenage daughter's achievements. She was a soccer player, and apparently she was a very good one because the basement was overflowing with awards.

What I saw in Doug at that moment was a man who was looking for someone to celebrate with him. He was proud of his daughter. He wanted to share his stories and all he needed was another person who was willing to listen. He wanted someone to see and experience what his daughter had accomplished. Doug began telling me about how much potential his daughter had and how far he would have to drive so that she could be part of an all-star group and enter into better tournaments. The stories may have been a little skewed with bias or blind hope, but nevertheless, this day was a day for Doug to celebrate and he wanted someone to share it with him.

This incident with Doug is an example of how I learned to think wider and make new connections. Reimagining is really the practice of expanding our approach to our routines and our daily lives beyond ourselves to include others in meaningful ways. It can be as simple as me sharing a World Cup soccer game with my elderly neighbour. I didn't plan to celebrate his daughter's achievements with him, but I did extend friendship and place myself in a position to make a genuine connection with someone who may have needed it. These simple ways of reimagining can lead to profound stories. It chips the edges away from our tunnel vision and offers new space for connection and conversation and relationships to grow.

I wouldn't have imagined that when I went to visit Doug during the soccer game, I was actually being led to a man who needed to celebrate with someone. It showed me, though, how important it is to remain open to reimagining the ordinary as an opportunity and to remain open, myself, to being a "living sacrifice." If we live present among our neighbours, we can more easily see where God is moving and join in with what he is building in our communities.

These days, I've pushed this concept of reimagining further. I notice people who have different gifts to offer. A woman who lives down the road makes spices. Another neighbour is a hunter with an overflowing freezer. There's a man who owns a boat and all kinds of tackle. As a way of reminding myself to reimagine what community is like within our neighbourhood, we began to share our gifts with each other. I would take the coffee that I had roasted, appropriately branded "Good Neighbour Coffee," and offer it as a gift to people in my community. Weeks later, those people would come to us and say: "our freezer is so full. Would you like any breakfast sausages?" The lady with the spices would come to me and ask if I'd taste them and give some feedback. The man with the boat took us fishing because it filled him to share his passion with others. I always accept these kinds of offers.

As much as this may sound like the old bartering system, it is really a practice that unearths a new way of existing in community. It is a rhythm of practice that we can implement to shape a beautiful connection within our neighbourhoods. This is the community that Christ has called us to be: sharing with and loving each other without conditions or expectations. This way of living calls us to shift our perspective in order to enrich the souls of others and, in that process, we fill our own souls as well.

THE PRACTICE OF HOSPITALITY

Hospitality is a practice that is scattered consistently throughout the pages of scripture. It is a theme that quietly repeats itself and is often incorporated in the stories that Jesus tells, or in the way he teaches his disciples. In the book of Acts, the gift of hospitality is an integral part of the formation of the church. Paul encourages us in Romans chapter 9 to love with sincerity, to show hospitality, and to treat those who mistreat you with great love.

When it comes to relationships, we are told that we must extend hospitality to others. Some people think that they are not naturally good at hospitality and, therefore, they shy away from it. The heart of hospitality, though, is not about whether or not you are good at it. It simply starts with what you have to give. It is about what you can offer to another person. It is about creating space and inviting others to share it with you. This is what Romans 12 is talking about when it says we should give ourselves as an offering to others in light of God's mercy. Hospitality is a beautiful and foundational way to experience God and love on His people.

Many stories outline the idea of coffee shops, hair salons, bookstores, bars, and other places that people go to hang out as the heart of community. In most cities that have healthy communities, you will find places like that. They are spaces that connect people and, inherently, they offer hospitality. Hospitality is, fundamentally, when someone understands what they have to give, is willing to offer it, and invites people to gather and share in it as well.

I met a man, once, who told me an amazing story from his childhood. He said that he used to have neighbours who told their children that they would always make enough food, every dinner, for two extra guests. The children did not need to ask permission to invite someone over but, rather, were challenged to be proactive in welcoming others to their home and their table. There were many nights where no guests would come and, in that case, the extra food would be used for lunches the next day or the leftovers would be creatively incorporated into other meals. But, regardless, every dinner was made with the expectation that there would be two extra people sharing their table.

The man who told me this story was a recipient of one of these invitations. As a neighbour, he was often invited by the children to come over for dinner. They would tell him that their mother was expecting him and that she was always counting on extra people. These statements must have felt so inviting, so inclusive.

What those children had to give was an invitation. What that neighbour received was a place where he felt welcomed. He experienced a version of hospitality within that healthy household that went above and beyond the norm. This neighbourhood had an amazing sense of community, simply because these parents challenged their children to invite others to their dinner table. They instilled this mentality into their children. They taught them that this was the normal way to do life, and it blessed the entire community. Hospitality changes the rhythm and the feel of a neighbourhood.

This story is true story number twelve on the back of my packages of Good Neighbour Coffee. Coffee roasting is a creative hobby I began to explore as a way to share a gift with my neighbours and, eventually, I turned it into a small business. This is where the name Good Neighbour Coffee came from. I have a couple of different roasts, I play around with the way I serve it to people, and on the back of the packaging I include true stories of people making change in their communities by being good neighbours.

This coffee is a gift that I have to offer. It is something that I can bring to the table. I share my coffee with my neighbours often, and I encourage them to share the coffee with their neighbours as well. I'm not doing this out of a motivation for more revenue, but more as a way to creatively explore how to use a gift to share and develop community.

Food is another gift that is often centrally connected to the practice of hospitality. On one occasion, my wife and I decided that we wanted to bless a couple with whom we had been building a relationship for some time. We had heard that the woman had just undergone an intense knee operation and she was going to be bedridden for the next couple of weeks. The couple also had young children and my wife and I thought that we would make lasagna for them to take care of at least one meal that week. My wife makes very good lasagna. This is her gift and she can literally bring it to the table. We told the couple that we were making them lasagna and asked which night of the week they would like to have it.

"Why are you doing this?" they asked.

We told them that we knew about the knee operation and that, sometimes, in the midst of seasons like this, cooking a meal can be just one more extra chore. We wanted to alleviate some pressure and extra work and bless them with food. They told us that Thursday would work best.

When we brought the meal, the woman was sitting on the couch, unable to move, but the children were home. They let us into the house. Even though we had told the family that we were coming, the lasagna was still a pleasant surprise to them because we had actually acted on our promise. The family was grateful, but they asked, again, why we did this for them.

At this point, I recognized that this question was an "open door." I thought quickly about the best way to respond. I had already established a bit of a relationship with these people and I fully intended on carrying the relationship further so this made me see that their question of "why" was an invitation to something deeper. The way I answered this question could turn into a meaningful conversation. It was a pivotal moment.

I explained to them that we had gifts that we wanted to use to bless people. I said that, because we were neighbours, sharing these gifts and welcoming each other could only enhance our community.

The mother was extremely grateful and, weeks later, her husband came to drop off the dish that we had brought the lasagna in. This meeting gave us another opportunity to engage in conversation and that conversation gave me an indication of where more "open doors" might exist in our relationship with this family. The motivation for doing this was only to show love, as Christ commands us. Understanding this motivation within our own hearts when it comes to loving our neighbour is crucial. It is important that we are not trying to get them to go anywhere with us. We shouldn't place expectations on our neighbours or try to solicit them into some type of response. We must not love with ulterior motives. We are simply told to love others unconditionally, as Christ loved us.

Not long after we shared that lasagna, another neighbour of ours had to foreclose his house. Within a few months, the house had renters in it. Although it was a slightly awkward situation, the renters were new to the community and we felt compelled to extend hospitality to them as well. On the day they moved in, I knocked on the door to say hello. I had brought a package of Good Neighbour Coffee with me, medium blend, already ground. When they opened the door, I said, "Welcome to the neighbourhood! I roast coffee and I thought I'd bring a package over to you. I'd love to hear your feedback on it. I can always roast you up something different, if you'd prefer."

They told me that they didn't really drink much coffee but they appreciated the gesture. I said they could take it anyway, and I asked if they would be interested in attending our upcoming neighbourhood barbeque. We had a short conversation about the community, about what people did there and events that were happening. As we talked, they invited me into their house.

I told them that I didn't have a lot of time because my family was expecting me to be home for dinner shortly, but that I would come in for the amount of time I had available. They offered me a glass of water and I proceeded to sit down with the couple and their two young children, both under the age of five. They were still unpacking and they told me to excuse the mess and, as they did, they began to tell me a little more about themselves. They were from Scotland and they had just immigrated to Canada. They talked about some of the things that had happened to them back in Glasgow and, from their comments, I began to realize that these people had a faith background. It was clear that they had had roots in a church community that represented Christ. Based on this information, I asked if they were Christians. This was a bold move on my part, but I was also confident about what their answer would be from what I had gleaned from the evidence in some of their remarks.

In response to this question, the couple began to tell me about their story. They told me how they had been challenged in their faith and they also commented on the tradition that they had been brought up in and the differences they had encountered in a new country. What surprised me most, though, is what happened next.

They invited me to sing with them.

I couldn't believe that, fifteen minutes before, I had just knocked on this couple's door and now I was in their living room, holding a hymnbook, and singing with their family. We were a bit of an unconventional choir but, as our voices blended together, I saw a beautiful glimpse into the heart of this family. I also began to reflect on the different responses I'd encountered as I knocked on the doors of people in my community. On one hand, I thought of the family that we had delivered lasagna to, asking why on earth we would be so generous. This family, however, swept me across to the other end of the continuum. They had just moved into the community themselves and already they were extending hospitality to me, inviting me to sing with them in their living room. They had a whole history of understanding their faith and their role in God's mission.

These two families remind me that hospitality does not always unfold in the ways we dream or envision on the outset. When we open our doors, or see the doors of others open, and practice hospitality, we should not be surprised about what we encounter. It reminds me of the disciples in Luke 10 who met people that would welcome them in, serve them food, pray and sing with them, or even simply say "thank you" or ask "why." In the spirit and discipline of hospitality, we can see where God is at work and we can join him in that work as we move forward in our days.

THE PRACTICE OF VULNERABILITY

During the time I have spent actively trying to love my neighbours, I've discovered that one of the most powerful tools I can use to develop deeper connections with people is that of vulnerability. This goes deeper than some of the other practices I've talked about, and the beauty of it is that it does not require a special set of gifts that only belongs to certain people. Vulnerability is similar to confession. It creates the sense of equality or a level playing field between the people engaged in conversation. It invites others to let down their guard in a safe place. Relationships open to new depths in contexts where people feel as though they can be vulnerable without being judged or taken advantage of.

One time, on the day after Christmas, I went to a party at a neighbour's home. We sat together, eating food from a variety of different cultures and wandering through many different topics of conversation. One discussion in particular stood out that night. We began to talk about the hockey game that was on TV, which led to a conversation about where some of the different players were originally from. Eventually we began to talk about different countries and places where we had personally travelled. I mentioned that my wife and I had recently visited Israel and seen many of the places that are written about in the Bible and that had, more recently, been in the news. We began to talk further about the scriptures, and the conversation eventually drifted toward the topic of forgiveness.

The people in the group knew that forgiveness was a theme in the scriptures, but they also expressed the difficulty of actually being a forgiving person in their daily lives. This conversation naturally began to break into the territory of vulnerability as we shared our struggles in this area. The husband in the couple who were hosting the party told me that he had been brought up to forgive and forget, yet he was constantly challenged in the actual practice of this.

The more personal stories you share, the deeper you go. A conversation suddenly gains a different level of meaning when someone opens up in honesty about a struggle or a question. At this Christmas party, we realized that when one person is vulnerable, it invites others to be real as well. It would be discouraging if just one person was vulnerable about their struggle with forgiveness and everyone else in the room jumped in as saviors, trying to fix the problem as if we held all of the answers. The practice of vulnerability allows us to join the conversation and share our challenges alongside each other.

This is really an organic form of Bible study. At that Christmas party, no one was pulling out a Bible or referencing key scriptures, but we were discussing a relevant struggle in our lives that connected deeply to the teachings of Jesus and what we believe he commanded us to live out in practice. It had naturally evolved out of our previous conversations. Two of us had opened up honestly about our struggles, and that first step allowed others in the room to feel comfortable enough to contribute and share as well. We weren't trying to correct each other or offer magical answers. It was simply a space to share together and listen to one another. Sometimes the greatest encouragement is the knowledge that we are not alone in our struggles, and sometimes the greatest affirmation is feeling as though we are being heard.

The best story I have to illustrate the practice of vulnerability is my neighbour Alex, the one whose story I shared earlier about dealing with anger. Alex does not know much about the scriptures. He does not know much about who Jesus is and what he has taught. Some might call his lifestyle a little rough. Over the course of the time that we were neighbours, I befriended him enough to realize that he struggled with anger in his life.

This is what happened. Alex got a bunch of gravel sprayed onto his lawn when the road was being cleaned up. He wanted to get the gravel off as soon as possible so he could mow his lawn again. I offered to help him because I had a tool that would get the job done easily and efficiently. When we were finished with our task, we sat back with a drink in his garage and began to talk. His garage was filled with posters that told me a little about the story of his life. I didn't necessarily agree with this lifestyle, but I could tell from the posters that Alex had no problem celebrating it. I also knew that I had enough background relationship with Alex that it wouldn't be inappropriate to guide the conversation into a little more personal territory at this point. After a bit of small talk about how well the tool had worked, I steered the discussion in a new direction. I asked him, with a humble spirit: "Do you ever get angry?" He said that he did, which I already knew. I followed his answer with another question, edging toward a deeper level of vulnerability. "So do I," I said. "I struggle with it."

Then I asked: "What do you think I should do about it?"

I had opened up to a point where I knew he could relate to me, and where I knew I could relate to him. I took the first step and allowed myself to, in a way, be placed on a table for "open-heart surgery." For two men sitting by the driveway and sharing drinks after doing yard work, this kind of discussion isn't exactly normal or generally expected. The conversation, however, continued and began to lead us toward more open doors as he answered my questions. He shared his own struggles with anger and how he attempted to deal with it. If a third person was listening in, the conversation would have sounded rather light, but between us as men, it was actually a deep and even spiritual discussion because we were practicing rare and honest vulnerability.

These little opportunities usually don't just happen by themselves. We have to exercise a certain amount of assertion and alertness to recognize how God works. We also have to be engaged in prayer over these things, asking God to lead the way and open the doors or provide the opportunities and the words to say. It may not be effective every time. We may not always be confident about what we should say or how to respond. Regardless of these potential reservations, though, the practice of vulnerability is vital to cultivating deeper relationships. The best news is that it is a muscle that we can strengthen over time.

Fear often gets in the way of vulnerability. It can stop us from asking a deeper question. Sometimes we don't know our place in the conversation, so we keep quiet. However, vulnerability has a special kind of ability to connect and even to heal. We must take the step of faith and be willing to venture into honesty. Your story may be more powerful than you realize.

It is in another neighbourhood, where a couple named Jim and June live out this practice of vulnerability in beautiful ways. On a summer morning in July 2014, Jim and June woke up very early to discover that their neighbour's house was on fire. The fire had started in the garage and June, recognizing that the flames were totally out of control, ran over to the house to wake up the neighbours. June had been working to establish a relationship with this family beforehand, and she bravely went into the house without hesitation. When the family got safely out of their home, it began to burn all the way down to the ground. The outrageous flames grew larger and began to spread to the two houses on either side, one of which was Jim and June's home. The three families, as well as the rest of the neighbourhood who had gathered to witness the disaster, stood on the sidewalk and watched as all three homes burned completely to the ground in fourteen minutes.

What happened that day was absolutely devastating. Jim and June had been deeply engaged in their community, building relationships with their neighbours. Now they were in a position of desperate need. They were displaced from their home, starting from scratch, and needed a community to surround them. Jim and June had helped me think through the concept of practically loving our neighbourhoods, and when I heard about their situation, I was shocked. As time progressed, they struggled to reconstruct their life, planning next steps and starting over. They assured us, though, that they planned to stay in the same neighbourhood. They wanted to rebuild in their old community.

Months passed by, and gradually Jim and June began to piece their lives back together. What surprised me, though, as I watched them journey through this situation, was that Jim and June were still thinking of ways to creatively love their community despite all that they had lost. One day, in October, they approached me to ask if they could possibly borrow a table, as well as a coffee pot, some coffee, and an extension cord. When I asked them why they needed these things, they told me that they wanted to use Halloween night as an opportunity to bless their neighbours. They wanted to set up the table at the end of their driveway to offer coffee and treats to the people in the community.

This act of love made me a little emotional when I realized how openly loving and vulnerable they were being despite the difficult circumstances they were living in. Even though their house had burned down, they were still willing to grasp opportunities to bless their neighbours. They served the coffee at the end of their driveway, in front of the ashes and remnants of their burned home. This was a striking visual picture of vulnerability.

One by one, on Halloween night, neighbours came by. Some cried because they loved Jim and June, and the tragedy of what they lost was so tangibly obvious. Jim and June knew that people long for depth of relationship and they knew the power of actively loving others despite the difficulty of their personal circumstances. In fact, because they were open about the difficulty of their personal circumstances and still offered hospitality and love in the midst of that, their community was profoundly touched. They created a space for people to come alongside in the hard places. Jim and June served out of a sense of gratitude and told everyone that they planned to rebuild in the next year. At the time of this writing, they are preparing to move into their new house very soon.

The depth of that Halloween night emphasizes that we all have something to offer. Even though it may be difficult, being honest and real is exactly the quality of people we are called to be as Christians, especially when we study the life of Jesus Christ and follow his teaching in the scriptures.

Thank you, Jim and June, for your willingness to love so openly in such a beautifully vulnerable way.

THE PRACTICE OF INVESTMENT

The other day we switched investors. This required us to sit down with the new person in charge to discuss our financial past and map out a plan for the future. At the beginning of the conversation, the investor asked one question: "where do you want to be?" Essentially, he was asking us how we wanted to retire. He wanted to know what age we planned to retire at and how much money we wanted to retire with. He was gaining an idea of what steps we'd need to take to get from where we were now to where we wanted to be in the future.

As we were speaking to the investor, and as he continued to ask us questions, I found myself drawing comparisons in our conversation with the practice of loving your neighbour. One of the questions that the investor asked was "what do you have to offer?" The investor needed to know the answer to this question because, if we were borrowing our money, it wouldn't have made sense for us to invest it. The bank would never lend you money if it couldn't make as much as you could in investing it. They will always make sure that their money-making ventures trump yours. The investor wanted to know what money was available. What did we have to invest?

This idea is very similar to the concept of neighbouring. When we invest in our neighbours, it is not about giving up beyond our means. Rather, it is about assessing what we already have to offer.

When we outline the needs of a community, we gain an idea of areas that are lacking. It may reiterate obvious gaps and problems that may need to be addressed. However, outlining a checklist of needs may not be enough to engage the rest of the community to fix these issues. Simply acknowledging the issues is not always a motivation to initiate a process of change. Usually there is already a certain amount of awareness of these problems. The question to propose, however, flips this idea around and, instead of pointing out gaps, it fills the hands of the community. It is a way of empowering a neighbourhood though highlighting the assets they already possess that may potentially be used to enhance the community and fill in some of those areas of lack. Some people might have the asset of time to give, some might have money, but we must encourage ourselves to think beyond this and view our assets more creatively.

In our community, one neighbour is a hunter and, therefore, his freezer is always overflowing with meat. Another woman makes spices. I roast coffee. Another gentleman owns a fishing boat and loves to take others along on his fishing trips. Another neighbour is a gifted conversationalist and mediator. She has the ability to give wise insights and solve problems that may arise between people. The list goes on.

One time we were out walking in our community because I wanted to bring some freshly roasted coffee to one of the neighbours, as I often do. I had strategically and prayerfully chosen this particular house to visit that day and when I offered the woman the coffee, she accepted it gratefully. As I stood in her doorway, I happened to notice that, behind her, there were many plants that she had begun to grow. This was January, so I knew that she couldn't plant them out in the garden yet. "What are you doing with all of those plants?" I asked. I recognized that the place where she lived did not have enough room for her to put all of these plants in a garden. I started thinking that I had more than enough space in my garden, and an idea began to form. She told me that she loved to grow things but she didn't have enough space to put all of the plants, and that is why they filled her living room. She voiced concern about what she was going to do with all of those plants. She knew that they were growing far too large and that many would outgrow their pots by the time she would get an opportunity to put them in the ground.

When I heard that, I asked if there were any plants that I could buy, or if there were any that she wanted to plant in the space in our backyard, listing off some possible options for her to think over. She did think about it and, over the course of that year, she invested in both those plants and our lives by accepting the offer to share our garden.

This story is beautiful to me because I came in with no expectations. I was simply creatively thinking about investment and what I might have to offer this woman in her plant dilemma. Thinking about creative investment is a valuable practice for all of us to engage in. We might not always feel confident about what we have to offer on the outset, but we should still explore our possibilities. We've all been given gifts and skills from God, and he gives these gifts to us with the purpose of investing in other people.

Similar to making a financial investment, intentionally investing in our neighbourhoods requires us to evaluate what we have to offer and think about unique ways to use those assets for others. The word "investment" implies that there is a certain amount of return that is expected. This return might not just be a personal benefit, either. It has the potential to enhance the lives of the people we are choosing to invest in as well, and this contributes to the greater whole.

Gardening with the neighbour woman was an avenue that allowed us to develop a relationship. We began to understand that this was about far more than gardening, and as we exchanged what we had to offer, the relationship grew into something that was deeply valuable to all of us. Her husband was a hunter and their freezer was always overflowing with meat. Eventually, we started to trade the coffee that I roasted in exchange for some of the meat in their freezer. As our relationship deepened and expanded, we began to see different angles and perspectives into each other's lives. We talked about the delicate process of smoking meat. We found out that this couple had restored an old car. Eventually, our conversations ventured into deeper territory, talking about death and pain.

There was a depth and beauty to that relationship that paralleled the organic beauty of the plants we were caring for in the garden. It began to spill over into the larger community as well. For their son's birthday, the couple decided to get a giant slip and slide and invited others in the neighbourhood to use it along with them. This wasn't an organized program for the community or city. It was simply a group of neighbours gathering to fly down a steep hill on a heavy grade plastic, riding the edge of danger and safety together. At the end of the slip and slide was a ramp that might shoot you two feet into the air and land you in the pool. Your chances of actually making it into the pool were entirely determined by weight. If you were a bit too heavy, you ran the risk of overshooting the pool. If you were too light, you might not make it up over the ramp with enough velocity and, therefore, fall short of the pool.

This afternoon was not only fun, but also it made beautiful memories in our community that neighbours still talk about today. All we needed to bring that day was a willing spirit and it paid us back in the relationships we built together and the sense of community that developed from this casual event. We often pass by this couple in our neighbourhood and we continue to ask questions, continue conversations, and maintain our investment in each other's lives. One day, while we were walking, the woman stopped by and rolled down her car window to chat about the day. She had platters of food in the back of her car to take to an event, which we noticed over the course of our conversation. Later that night, she came over and told us that one of the platters of food hadn't been touched. She said that she wanted to give it to us to enjoy along with our children. The point of this story is not that we personally benefitted from this kind gesture, but that she had thought of us. It told us how valuable and beautiful our relationship was as neighbours to her. All of this had come out of sharing a garden plot together.

To be thought of, as we were in receiving the platter of food from our neighbour, is a rich experience. However, this gesture was the result of previous time and intentional investment into our relationship for months prior. Today we have tea with her regularly and we sit down and talk about her husband's job change or the new juicer that she bought or living sustainably or raising children. She is quite a bit younger than my wife and I, so we are coming from different stages of life and we have had many different life experiences, but when we come together we always find common ground. Gardening and tea and food have been avenues that lead us to each other's celebrations, and, sometimes, sharing of pain. We don't do this as a chore. We do this because we know the beauty that unfolds when we practice the art of investment.

One of my neighbours came to me with a confession after hearing about this practice of investing in others. He knew a person who lived next door quite well and this neighbour had invited him over one afternoon to watch the Ultimate Fighting Championships over a beer. My neighbour told me that he actually hated Ultimate Fighting and beer. He told me that he liked to keep his Sunday afternoons to himself. He said, however, that because he had been invited, he could probably tolerate half an hour of fighting and maybe pass on the beer in favour of something else in order to love his neighbour by showing interest. On a grand scale, this would be a small investment compared to the possible return of building a new relationship and gaining a sense of greater community.

I often say that invitation is 50% of ministry. This may seem daunting to some, at first. However, the practice of investment begins with invitation. We need to live with eyes open and alert to possible ways we can include and invite people to participate in these practices alongside us. We need to be alert to what gifts they might be able to contribute. To shy away from these opportunities or to deliberately not invite others would rob the other person of a blessing. If a person comes to mind, there is a reason for that. We must pay attention to these promptings and ideas that rise in our minds. We must take that step beyond thinking about others and reach out to ask them to join in. Once we ask, though, we need to go a step further and tell them why we want them to join, why we feel as though they could contribute well, why we thought of them specifically to participate. They may decline your invitation, but you may have still blessed them by affirming their value. When you think of others and invite them, you are communicating that they have gifts and talents worth investing. Sharing this with each other is a way to cultivate rich communities.

THE PRACTICE OF TRUST

The theme of trust or, more specifically, broken trust, seems to be threaded through most of our lives. This is a topic that often carries a certain weight of anxiety along with it. Usually people speak from experience when they talk about broken trust, and these stories are often painful memories. It takes courage to trust, and it also requires vulnerability. When trust is broken, it can be deeply wounding. The scriptures tell us that in order to live a life of depth, though, trust is absolutely required. Lack of trust can cause division and tension within a community and it does not cater to healthy relationships. Since trust is such a delicate thing, it usually needs to be initiated by one person and carefully built up with persistent consistency. Again, there is no particular agenda involved in the practice of trust. It is motivated from a place of love.

The idea of trust is one that some people try to avoid out of fear. One time, when I was involved in setting up a series of block parties within my city to help other neighbours connect, I stumbled upon this practice of trust in a very practical way. It occurred to me, through this experience, how little trust we actually extend to one another within our communities and how much we tend to withhold it in daily life.

The idea of block parties in our city had begun to gain momentum and, as we did more of them, they presented wonderful opportunities to develop community. I wrote a letter to the city leaders, hoping to that they would support the idea. I wanted the block party invitations to come from them, the governing body, rather than from one relatively unknown individual. The city did eventually collaborate with me to set up these block parties. I was appointed as the "go between," as the person who would set up these parties and oversee them in order to develop healthier connections within communities. It became a movement within our city.

We were given a stainless steel trailer barbeque built by a manufacturer approved by the food service industry. I had happened to come across a man who had one for sale and gave it to me at a quarter of the price of what they cost new. This was a gift to us, and I started to brainstorm how I could use this new tool to bring my neighbours together under the banner of love. What I didn't know was that this tool would also play a role in helping me understand this practice of trust.

The eighth block party that I initiated happened at the corner of two main roads and we planned to set up the barbeque in a neighbour's front yard. Generally, my practice is to simply remain available while these parties are going on. I set up the barbeque and we leveled it and, as we worked at this, we had conversations about how I got the barbeque, which always leads me into deeper discussion.

What I hadn't anticipated on this day was a call from my wife. She asked me if I could pick up our youngest daughter from her swimming lesson. I told her that I was at a block party and that it would be very difficult for me to just leave in the middle of it. She told me that someone needed to get our daughter. I said that I would see what I could do.

I hung up the phone and went back to the guys by the barbeque. I told them about the phone call and that I might not be able to stay at the block party for as long as I had hoped to. I explained that because I had to pick up my daughter from swimming lessons, I'd have to leave them the keys for the lock on the barbeque trailer hitch. I asked them if they would hold it for me because I wouldn't be able to pick it up until the next morning.

They looked at me. "Are you kidding?" they asked.

At first I thought that they didn't want to hold the trailer for me, but I quickly realized that, rather than denying my request, they were surprised that I trusted them enough to keep the trailer. They were shocked that I would leave a $14 000 barbeque with them when we had no pre-established relationship. One man asked bluntly, "you're just going to trust us with this? That's not the way the world works." I was happy that he had voiced this concern, but I was also disappointed by the truth of this statement. It was a sad statement about the way our communities exist and function today. There's a fundamental, assumed distrust of strangers: a pattern that has ingrained itself into our minds, our behaviours, and our perception of people.

This situation opened a new door that I did not anticipate. It is true that our neighbourhoods are generally void of this essential element of trust. Our experience of community is often one of suspicion, or distance until trust is earned. I did leave the barbeque there overnight and I did pick it up in the morning. That short conversation, though, left me with a deeper understanding of how important, and how abnormal, it is for us to practice trust: both giving and receiving it.

I believe that most people want to be trusted and we can all take hold of small opportunities to offer this trust. In a previous chapter, I told a story about a woman who shared our garden over the course of a year and through the relationship that we built with her, we allowed her to go into our home to feed our pet birds while we were away. This required a great deal of trust on our part, since we were twelve hours away from our house at the time, but we were willing to offer it because we knew it would mean a lot to her. We could have chosen a number of other neighbours, but we decided to ask this woman as an opportunity to intentionally forge trust within our relationship. We told her how to enter our house and explained what exactly needed to be done.

I believe that there is a value to trust and we can exercise it in many areas of our lives. One area, however, where trust is particularly difficult to extend for many people is the area of money. One time, during the Christmas season, I wanted to invest in some of the neighbours. Through some of the connections I had been making I noticed that there was one particular person who bought a product via catalogue. I thought it would be convenient for her to order some things for me so I could surprise my wife with a few gifts. She was willing to do this for me and it became an interesting opportunity because, the way the situation unfolded, I ended up needing to prepay her in the sum of $50. We had a bit of a pre-existing relationship to leverage this trust. The woman was honoured, not just to do this favour for me, but also that I trusted her enough to give her the money ahead of time.

These are small, but genuine and deeply meaningful practices that we can implement with alertness to see and hear opportunities to creatively initiate trust within our communities among our neighbours whom we are asked to love.

THE ART OF CONVERSATION

For most people who are learning to intentionally love their neighbours, it can be difficult to know how to initiate conversations. Many people get hung up on what to say and how to say it. Sometimes fear and anxiety holds a person back from engaging in conversation because their neighbours are not associated with them in any area of life other than living in close proximity to one another.

The mind is sometimes tricky to reign in. Mental posture, however, is fundamental to the art of conversation. There is a certain amount of training and preparation we must undergo in the area of discipleship as we seek to live out these practices of loving our neighbours. Controlling our mindset is the first step in the act of love.

As a professional broadcaster, I was trained, in a number of different ways, how to speak to people. Public speaking was one element of the training, but what I learned from the techniques taught within the booth radically shifted my perspective. When you broadcast, you are talking to people, but you are essentially carrying on the conversation as a monologue in a room by yourself. This, along with speaking into a microphone, which isn't normally present during casual conversation in real life, can make it difficult to establish a connection with the audience without employing some mental techniques.

In the broadcasting world you are trained to talk in a personable way, even though you are addressing the masses that you cannot see. In training, we were taken into a room where we were told to record ourselves and listen to the playback. We did this to understand how our inflections and the way we spoke changed as a result of our mental posture at that time. Some simple techniques they taught us was that when you talk into a microphone, you must know that you sometimes come across as someone who is talking to the masses, even though the goal is to make it a more personal experience for the listener. One technique we were taught was to put a picture of our mom on the microphone. When we imagined that we were speaking to our mothers, rather than a crowd of unknown faces, the tone of the conversation immediately changed. As a result, the listener feels more connected to the announcer's voice. Subtle shifts in mentality or phrasing, even switching from saying "hello out there!" to a simple "how are you doing?" changes the tone of speech. It alters the spirit of the conversation.

Just like training for a sport, training ourselves in the art of mental posture within our conversations is absolutely necessary. Scripture is constantly telling us to be prepared. Be prepared to respond, as Peter says in 1 Peter 3:15. I recommend seven areas to focus on to develop this mental posture and may help guide us toward better conversations with our neighbours.

1. **Know and act as if the Kingdom of God is here**: The Kingdom of God is already present with us. Although it isn't displayed in its fullness, yet, we catch glimpses of it now and then. Someday it will be seen in full completion. Since we have that hope and that anticipation, we must live out the reality that Christ is Lord. He rules. Therefore, how we talk and how we act must reflect this truth that we believe.

When a parent sends their young child to school on the first day on the bus, there is a certain amount of anxiety and concern involved. To reassure the child, the parent's demeanor tends to shift as they confidently tell them not to worry. The parent's actions reflect what they know to be true: the child will be fine. They don't want to validate the child's anxiety through their body language or tone of voice. Although the child might be unsure, the parent can assure him that, throughout history, the first day of school has been predominantly a positive experience for most people.

That child will go off to school with his parent's assurance in his mind. In this way, he has been mentally prepared for this experience from someone he trusted. Likewise, when we prepare mentally for loving our neighbours, our attitude, our words, and our actions should be reflective of what we believe.

2. **Listen and hear**: Many people in our society, at least in North American culture, do not feel heard. This is a root problem that has perpetuated into a number of larger issues that beg to be resolved. Deep problems arise when people do not feel as though anyone is listening to them. This is so important, and part of the art of conversation includes intentionally preparing ourselves for listening. Personally, I know that I love to talk and share my thoughts. I need to work extremely hard to listen and truly hear people.

When I do make the effort to listen well, though, it usually only produces good things. One example of this is when, one day, a mother in our neighbourhood approached me. I had witnessed an earlier incident where her son had gotten picked on. The son had seen me as a witness, so I knew what was coming when the mother approached me. She was upset about the injustice that had taken place with her son. When I saw her coming, I immediately knew that I had to prepare for the art of conversation. I could have said multiple different things to this woman, but the most important thought that kept running through my head was that I needed to hear her out. I needed to be willing to understand her perspective and validate it.

The son had somewhat been the cause of the teasing that had been inflicted on him. I can't say with integrity that he didn't deserve what had happened to him. In light of that, though, my preparation for the art of conversation was to address this mother on a couple of different levels. First, I needed to listen to what she had to say, even though she was upset and even though she was using fairly strong language. Second, I needed to ask questions of clarification so that I knew I had a clear understanding of what she was talking about. I already knew what she was saying, but I also understood that there was room for assumption in me that would be better to straighten out verbally. When I clarified that we were on the same page, she relaxed a little bit. Then, before she could launch into a description of what her son had told her about the incident, I beat her to the punch and began to outline some of the details that I knew she would address. When she heard me describe these things, she realized that I understood her point of view. I could hear where she was coming from.

The point of this story is that the power of listening and hearing is an element of conversation that helps guide us into more positive and biblical areas as agents of change. The mother approached me with anxiety and strong language and emotion, but after twenty minutes she left with more joy and a new perspective because she felt heard. Listening and hearing is the first step in taking the art of conversation seriously.

3. **You don't need to fix the problem**: There's a tendency in our culture toward solving or fixing things. We feel as though we have a responsibility to remedy situations. When there is a problem amongst neighbours, we feel tension, which, in turn, we feel obligated to diffuse. These can be tricky waters to navigate.

Preparing to give an answer about the hope you have in Christ does not mean "answer every question" or "fix every situation." The Scriptures do not demand that we are to have all the answers. Perhaps we have become victims of culture that has set us to think we have failed if we have no response. Often we miss opportunities to love our neighbour because we are so fixated on fixing or solving or answering. In marriage counseling I lead this exercise where the couple has a list of three wishes for the other. When they ask for their wish the response usually falls under the category of answering or fixing, but rarely does the response fall under the category of 'active listening.' This suggests that we are not caring as much about what the other is trying to communicate as we are trying to simply fulfill or justify why we should not fulfill the wish. This stands true for our other relationships too! Our culture seems to dictate that answers and solutions are what we are after, when it seems to forgo the opportunity to love. Perhaps we should consider it more valuable to share the load and journey together. Christ himself came to enter into our lives and redeem us which is a different approach than just fixing or answering. Most of the time our opportunity to love our neighbours, as Jesus commanded, allows us to be shaped as much as it is to shape the one with the questions. And besides, how often do we desire to have answers or solutions over and above the relationship?

The biggest challenge is death. Everyone eventually knows someone who dies, and eventually will die themselves. It is a confrontational issue that many have dealt with with great difficulty. I have several neighbours who have experienced the death of a loved one. There is very little I can do when it comes to fixing or answering, but I can be present with love, struggling alongside them, celebrating and commemorating during our time as neighbours.

Even when it comes to problems that we think we are able to solve, we can feel helpless. A few marriages in our neighbourhood have dissolved. This creates tension and heartbreak! The truth is you are limited in what you are able to do. On one occasion, Evan and Shannon decided that they no longer wanted to be part of a throw away culture, so they came back together through great determination. I am not sure what the trick was that brought about the reconciliation, but it was not something I can tell you "worked." But on July 11, 2015, Evan and Shannon renewed their vows in their backyard, in which I was invited to participate.

The proper response is to give an answer for the hope we have in Christ. This may be challenging, but needs to be held as a legitimate response to the brokenness in the world. Today, Evan and Shannon sit down with me asking questions about the Bible and its application to life. Again, my response is not to answer all of their questions, but to wrestle with them through the grey areas of life, pointing to our Lord.

4. **Prepare yourself by seeing and hearing with eyes and ears that belong to God**: This means to avoid approaching a neighbour with an attitude of prejudice or stereotype and, rather, to see them as a creation of God. Granted, that creation may be broken, but, regardless, we must treat others as a person that God has made. I've discovered that the block parties I've attended or supervised seem to amend misconception in this area. I'll hear that, during the course of a block party, a stereotype surrounding a neighbour was broken because of the interaction with that person. Often, by engaging in a more personal relationship with our neighbours, the stereotypes start to make sense. Their behavior patterns may manifest as a result of other circumstances and may have nothing to do with the actual integrity of the person. Block parties reveal these little unnecessary injustices by bringing the community together. Instead of letting rumours and gossip fly, these block parties have the potential to produce healing and restoration in many neighbourhoods. In order to sidestep this problem altogether, though, we must approach others with the mindset of God and be willing to see them as God sees them, void of stereotypes.

Sometimes I'll gather together a few people from the community, or other people who are passionate about loving their neighbours, for a prayer walk. I often get questions about what these prayer walks look like. Some people are afraid that doing this in their own neighbourhood might make them look strange and, therefore, are slow to accept the idea as one they should practice. What I tell these people is that we always end the prayer walk with dessert at someone's home, whoever volunteers to host.

We typically gather our group in front of that person's home, at the beginning of the walk, to open with prayer. Then we walk around to observe the neighbourhood with the eyes and ears of God. We are to put perceptions, stereotypes, and gossip aside and instead focus on how God sees this community. We walk slowly. We do not speak negatively of the people we see. We walk with the eyes of God.

5. **Categories of conversation**: All conversations can fall under one of three categories: creation, fall and redemption. Some conversations are negative and some are positive. When a person has aspirations for their business or their child's future, this belongs in the "creation" category. When someone is complaining or is telling a story about brokeness or maybe a theft that occurred within the community, this belongs in the "fall" category. A story about restoring a car or necessary surgery would fall under the "redemption" category.

When we have a conversation with someone, it is helpful to think about what that person is saying and what category that person is speaking within. This can help us frame our conversations through the lens of Scripture, even when we are talking about something as simple as the weather (sunny, rainy, drought or storms). This helps us understand others' stories in a deeper way, and it also helps us share our own stories, too.

6. **Tell your story**: Even the shyest introvert has a story to be told. When and where it is told may vary. An introverted mother may come to life at a neighbourhood Pinterest party because of her passion for sewing. A quiet man may open up about his story while working under the hood of a car. This happened in our neighbourhood when a man who generally kept to himself began to spill over with stories while we spent time in his garage after attending an anniversary party of another neighbour together. I

had seen some restored cars in his garage and began to ask him questions about them. He began to tell stories, powerful ones, which fell into the categories of creation and redemption. They opened up new windows and doors of opportunity and allowed me to understand him in a deeper way. Storytelling is not just for extroverts. It is not just for those who are gifted in that area, either. Everyone has a story to tell; they just may not feel called to tell it all the time, or until they are in a certain space or situation. Storytelling is a tool that is both powerful and necessary within the art of conversation. We don't tell stories as a form of competition, but, rather, to attempt to engage in the stories of each other, to relate, and to show empathy.

7. **Dance with the Holy Spirit**: many of us may be out of practice in this area, but in the art of conversation, there may be certain things going on beneath the surface that we are not aware of. Dancing with the Holy Spirit is difficult to describe, but the best way to think about it is through the analogy of dancing. Dancing is sometimes difficult. You might need to take a few lessons at first and you might need to learn how to follow without stepping on the toes of your partner, but the more we dance with a person over time and start to feel their rhythm, the more synthesized and beautiful it becomes. It is a mystery, but the encouragement is that, through time and practice, this dance will become beautiful.

So, as we learn this Holy Spirit rhythm together, let's lace up our shoes, get out into our communities, and dance.

In addition, enjoy a few more simple stories from surrounding neighbourhoods:

A Jar of Jam

I've lived in my area of the city for a couple of years and have not made the effort to get to know my neighbours. Although I consider myself a people person, I find it difficult to go up to new people and introduce myself. There has to be a reason to get out there, at least that is what I feel. Well, this past year the cherries on our 3 cherry trees were prolific so I found myself out in the yard frequently picking the ripest cherries and leaving the others for subsequent pickings. One of the trees reached out past our fence into the neighbours yard and there were handfuls of ripe cherries begging to be picked. Since an elderly lady lived next door, I was quite sure she wouldn't pick them but an idea came to mind to go onto her yard and pick the fruit unreachable from my side of the fence. I would make up some jam and take a few jars of the preserves to thank her for letting me go onto her property and take what was rightfully hers. After the jam was finished I chose an afternoon I was available to pop by her place to deliver the goods. When she came to the door I explained what I had for her and she was reluctant to take the jam but did anyhow and invited me in for a visit. I didn't expect that but what a lovely time we had sharing a bit about our lives with each other. She invited me to come again for tea sometime and mentioned she would wave me in from the street when she saw me return from work someday. I look in expectation for an invitation and/or another opportunity to share life stories.

Woodworking genius in our midst!

As the coordinator for the Neighbourhood Watch program in Lacombe, I was delivering fliers to homes on my street. I passed by a lady who was also delivering materials to homes so started up a conversation with her. We exchanged information with each other and she invited me to her place to get an updated catalogue of her material. While standing at the entrance to her home I heard her husband asking her for a pencil he was looking for. In my assessment he sounded rather rough and her response quite respectful in not knowing where it was. As I looked around the back yard it was clear that someone had been very busy with woodworking projects. I commented upon the beauty of it and a few minutes later the man of the house came out. What a work of art! I exclaimed. A burly fellow he was, yet he willingly shared he was the one who had taken on the project after an accident had left him unable to continue working in construction. How quickly one's opinion changes! He no doubt had reason to be burly and rough having lost a job he obviously enjoyed but when complimenting him upon the beauty of his artwork, he was only too quick to share his story. He no longer appeared or sounded rough and burly but impassioned and appreciative of the recognition. He even invited me in to see some more of his handiwork which I declined until another time. Perhaps I should take him up on the offer now since a few months have passed.

Neighbours from afar

After living in our neighbourhood for two months some friends from
Africa came to stay with us. These friends were poor, rural farmers and
many people questioned our wisdom in inviting them to Canada. There
was concern that they would see our material wealth and not want to
return to their mud huts. At the end of their stay our friends told us that
they were looking forward to going home and that they would pray for us.
They said, "You are so poor. We have been at your house for three weeks
and not a single neighbour come over to greet us.

The Final Challenge

By now I hope you have been encouraged to dream of what your neighbourhood may become. Perhaps the stories have given you an imagination for where you live or permission to try something in your neighbourhood. The purpose of this book is to help you dream, in hopes of reclaiming and redeeming the place in which you live and have your being.

When I tell a story about my neighbourhood or someone else's neighbourhood, I usually hear a reaction along the lines of, "We don't live in a place like that!"or "That would never work by us!" or "You haven't met my neighbour!" I suppose the last response is not an invitation but an exasperation of how unruly one's neighbour can be. All in all, the comments that follow my invitation to be neighbourly seem to indicate an expectation that one needs to do what *I* do or what others have done. This couldn't be further from the truth. The expectation is that you pay an increasing amount of attention to what goes on in *your* neighbourhood, not for gossiping reasons, but to prepare yourself to initiate, invest, or receive from that community called your neighbourhood. There is some confusion here. Remember, this is not making you into a service provider, nor does it ask you to be motivated by reasons other than love. This may take a bit of getting used to since culture can train us in other ways; for example, our consumer culture can make us believe that we should get something in return. We must work hard at staying the course, building on the vision that this is the Kingdom which we all desire.

Here are a few suggestions that may help move you forward:

1. **Find a neighbour who is willing to partner with you.** This is someone who shares the vision of having a healthy neighbourhood.

Perhaps there is more than one, but these are the people who will add, not take away, from the journey into your neighbourhood. This may be a Christian (they believe in loving neighbours), or simply a person who is willing to work with you (a person of peace). Regardless, they are a lifeline and keep you from feeling alone in moving forward.

2. **Identify your neighbours and neighbourhood.** When I first started seriously considering my neighbours, I did not even know what that meant, until I got together with the neighbours I described in the first step to have some coffee and actually draw (map) our neighbourhood. This helped identify boundaries. This may not be the same for others, but that's OK. We even went as far as writing the info we knew that made up those who lived in our neighbourhood. This was very helpful for all of us and was a great excuse for getting together.

3. **Walk your neighbourhood.** This could be step one if you already have identified your neighbourhood. I do this alone, or with my wife and even with our children. We have walked with neighbours, and I have heard that some neighbours have found this to be the foundation of a somewhat regular gathering. Walking your neighbourhood allows you to observe the characteristics that make up where you live.

4. **Pray.** We do not need to wait for problems, pain or panic to motivate us to pray. Simply recognize that, statistically, the homes around you encompass beauty and brokenness. The home next to yours will have everything from joy to pain on any given day. Eventually, you will discover more specific details for prayer, but we all can start by praying, "Our Father, in Heaven, bless those kids during this exam time", or "be with the family whose car has obvious new damage", or "give us an understanding as to what to do with the party house across the street…may your Kingdom come and your will be done in our neighbourhood as it is in Heaven."

5. **Give.** This could be time, talents or treasure. Just pick one neighbour who you are led to believe may receive your gift (you may want to first pray this through). You may want to think about giving food or a bottle of wine, tickets that you possess, a benefit from your hobby, an invitation or a helping hand.

Be creative! Be genuine! And think more of your neighbours than of yourself. For more stories and ideas that spur us on to thriving neighbourhoods, follow along at www.rickabma.com or consider inspiring others by sharing your story.

Subscribe at:
www.rickabma.com

Support the mission through the online purchase of:
www.goodneighbourcoffee.ca

ABOUT THE AUTHOR

Raised on a dairy farm, the youngest of seven, Rick Abma eventually pursued a college education that brought him into the world of broadcasting. Following his radio career, he entered full time ministry as a youth pastor. During his twenty years as a pastor, one eye was consistently focused on the majority of people who never darkened the door of the church. In 2014, he resigned to become a full time missionary in his own backyard while consulting for other neighbourhoods. He currently creates disciples in various other neighbourhoods, works with city leadership, roasts and markets "Good Neighbour Coffee" and hosts a radio show that features the stories from his experiences. His neighbourhood is just west of Lacombe, Alberta.